Constructive Communication
in International Teams

iCom Team

Constructive Communication in International Teams

An Experience-Based Guide

Waxmann 2014
Münster • New York

This book was financially supported by the European Union's territorial cooperation program "European Territorial Co-Operation Austria-Czech Republic 2007-2013" under the EFRE grant M00171, project "iCom" (Constructive International Communication in the Context of ICT).

EUROPEAN UNION
European Regional
Development Fund

EUROPEAN TERRITORIAL CO-OPERATION
AUSTRIA-CZECH REPUBLIC 2007-2013
Gemeinsam mehr erreichen. Společně dosáhneme více.

Bibliographic information published by the Deutsche Nationalbibliothek
The Deutsche Nationalbibliothek lists this publication in
the Deutsche Nationalbibliografie; detailed bibliographic data
are available in the Internet at http://dnb.d-nb.de

Print-ISBN   978-3-8309-3025-9
E-Book-ISBN   978-3-8309-8025-4

© Waxmann Verlag GmbH, 2014
Postfach 8603, 48046 Münster

www.waxmann.com
info@waxmann.com

Cover design: Inna Ponomareva, Münster
Typesetting: Stoddart Satz- und Layoutservice, Münster
Print: Hubert & Co., Göttingen

Printed on age-resistant paper,
acid-free as per ISO 9706

MIX
Papier aus verantwortungsvollen Quellen
FSC® C016439

All rights reserved.
Printed in Germany
No part of this publication may be reproduced, stored in a retrieval system or transmitted in any form or by any means, electronic, electrostatic, magnetic tape, mechanical, photocopying, recording or otherwise without permission in writing from the copyright holder.

Table of Contents

Foreword 7

Preface 13

Introduction 15
    Fostering constructive communication while gaining
    domain-specific competence 19

Knowledge Transfer 43
    Connect the dots 45
    Knowledge grows from sharing 61

Learning Organization 73
    Every perspective is valuable 75
    The team is the most wonderful place to learn 87
    Transparency yields flow 105

Leadership 123
    Hold constructs flexibly 125
    Care for the atmosphere 141
    Enable creativity in teams 157

Constructive Communication 167
    Communication matters, cultivate it 169
    Meeting at eye level opens doors 183
    Hiding consumes energy: Untie and focus 197

More Agility through Technology 207
    Maximize the chance for success: Be agile 209
    Two steps ahead 221

Summary and Inspirations 231

Authors and Supporters 241

Constructive communication in international teams
Foreword by David Ryback, Ph.D.

What a novel idea! A book about interpersonal communication written by 12 authors who put their egos on the shelf and dive into sharing an enterprise that typically is limited to one, two or, at the most, three authors!

Born out of a desire to share their personal experiences, and creating a mind-melding that is extremely rare in book publishing, these pioneers have succeeded at innovating a process of collaboration which is obviously quite successful. Dealing with all the aspects of successful interpersonal communication in the context of leadership and technology, they make the process fun for both themselves and their readers – no easy task.

Forming as a group of colleagues making up the International Constructive Communication project (iCom) from two countries, these brave people allow not only for personal openness in their writing but also for a freedom to choose just how much openness each member decides to share at any particular time.

In the introduction, the authors describe the parameters of efficiency in teamwork, including transparent communication with few barriers, a sense of inclusion, and decentralized decision-making. On the surface, this may appear difficult to achieve, given that strong personalities in business typically come with equally strong egos. But Dr. Carl Rogers had a simple approach (Ryback, 1989). Just bring the team players into a room, close the door to assure privacy and focus, and then encourage them to engage in emotional transparency under the nurturing guidance of a strong/soft facilitator who is sufficiently emotionally secure with him/herself to ensure that emotional authenticity rules the day.

Hidden personality conflicts, previously swept under the rug, are gently revealed, allowing all to see one another's fears and vulnerabilities that formerly kept them from being totally honest and authentic. Given sufficient time and attention, these conflicts and other dynamics that kept subtle ideas from being fully expressed give way to a common emotional language that the team can now use to transcend barriers to effective communication. Only in this "team-centered" manner can the group reach its full potential, thought Rogers. And now, in this book, these twelve authors prove his point.

Using an "agile, creative process," the book begins with ideas voted on by the authors in democratic fashion, then assigning responsibilities for research, case studies, etc., and then moving on to create this exciting publication for IT managers and any others wanting to reach for the winning potential of their teams, even involving potential readers as "business-partner" authors in this "shared vision," all of this requiring a "high degree of transparency," to use the authors' own terms. Communication took place in face-to-face meetings or online, and always with as much openness as possible.

One of the accidental learnings, the authors discovered, was how agile management, in addition to planning and scheduling, requires an openness from the start of any project, so that all minds start from the same page, even the same first lines on that first page. Another gem is the re-discovery of the importance of complementarity of strengths of team members – how they can fit with one another in seamless fashion as they become more productive and efficient.

A major focus in this book is comparing the interface between people both in face-to-face communication and electronically. Group e-mails are notorious for low response rates. So what to do? The authors come up with a highly sensible solution: Pace the two modes in such a manner that the connection among the members stays strong. Allow the electronic option to follow the real-life one so that the rapport stays vivid and motivating. This easy solution has sticky characteristics all over it: It is so simple and obvious once we put our brains around it, and it makes sense emotionally as well. And, here's the winner: once the rapport is assured, through proper pacing of the two modes, then the electronic communication takes off as well. Now we have the best of both worlds! But the essential key here, point out the authors, is that all this starts (and continues) with personal openness and honesty in order to maintain a high level of personal interaction, paying the highest respect to each and to every perspective.

In one of the sections (Case 1 in *Every Perspective is Valuable*), the authors point out how over-discussing a decision can take too much time, be seen as annoying by the participants and even result in some disengaging from the process. This awareness of one shortcoming of "openness" is important. As a matter of fact, students of leadership recognize that some forms are more effective than others, and there appears to be agreement that the open, democratic styles are most effective, though not entirely without fault.

Daniel Goleman (2000) explored six styles of leadership and concluded that the strongest is an Authoritative style in which the leader invites others to "come along" and join him/her in mobilizing a strong vision. The Democratic style, which is the focus of this book, forging consensus through collaborative participation, inviting all thoughts, is also very positive, as are empathic relationship building (Affiliative) and developing others through empathy (Coaching). What clearly doesn't work, according to the research, is demanding that associates comply with the boss' commands (Coercive) or setting high standards of achievement without discussion (Pacesetting). So there is an exalted place for democracy in action, but the caveat is to be respectful of time and circumstances as well, so that there is flexibility to move from democratic process to decision-making when time is of essence.

That's where the leader's experience comes into play – to know that subtle difference, and to make the transition smoothly. This is what the authors found out in their Nov. 21st to 23rd, 2012 meeting at Masaryk University, needing someone to steer the process, according to Edith; to form a shared vision first, according to Renate; to reach a balance between the structured and unstructured, according to Antonio; and to have minor decisions made by the leader/manager, according to Christina. As the subtitle, *Hold constructs flexibly* (in the **Leadership** category) implies, human interaction is too complex to expect one construct to fit all possibilities. This is true of facilitation as well, even when the aim is to hear all voices.

Carl Rogers himself seemed to have a built-in detector for discriminating between the need for openness to others' feelings and opinions on the one hand, and his own sense of determination to get things done a certain way, on the other. Driven, I believe, by a strong sense of fairness and respect for others, including a magical sense of group movement, he was able to make it safe for others to take the risk of personal openness to a surprising level. If there were any hints of annoyance or frustration at too much "democratic quibbling," he might be the first to express this, allowing the group to use this new awareness to move in a more productive (and perhaps less democratic) mode. It was this ability of his to express the nuances of feeling – whether his own or others' in the group, or the dynamic of the entire group – that made his leadership so charismatic, despite his humble personality. People could trust his sense of emotional awareness to the overall dynamic, buoyed by his unconditional respect for the benefit of the whole.

I have been surprised, over the years, as to how difficult this sense that characterizes Rogers has been to put into the books describing his style. It's easy to write about his emotional sensitivity; it's much more challenging to account for the expression of his inner drive to make things work with the strongest devotion to fairness and caring for others. Perhaps this is one of the unique strengths of this engaging book – to illustrate, through personal discussion and honest revelation, how to work with people in a compassionate way and, at the same time, deal with the challenges that arise in real-life situations that, at first blush, may seem to contradict the main theory but, in reflection, prove the theory by allowing for the exceptions, and then how best to deal with them.

Perhaps it does take a "jury" of twelve authors to form the strength to admit when an advocated approach fails, and how – in their collective opinion – these "errors" offer the opportunity to refine the applied theory, so that its applications to the real worlds of education and industry can take hold and offer the most productive outcomes.

Finally, when it comes to personal sharing, there are sometimes situations in which the path becomes frustrating because someone may have an agenda that appears incompatible with the group's collective expectations. Perhaps it would be helpful to have some guidelines here. Would it be appropriate to invite group members to share what: 1) each feels deeply, 2) is relevant to the discussion at hand, and 3) with an awareness of how the sharing might be received by the group members. Such guidelines might help in Case 2 of the *The Team is the Most Wonderful Place to Learn* section, as well as other cases through the book.

Ultimately, conclude the authors, what it comes down to is to learn to listen deeply and to be open to ongoing experience. This takes courage. As this book tackles the challenges in larger industrial organizations, from offering innovation time for greater creativity to communicating ideas across levels of leadership, the necessary courage becomes even more daunting. The terms "co-actualization" and "constructive-constructivist conversation" refer to mutual contribution to learning (Motschnig-Pitrik, 2008), relationships (Motschnig-Pitrik & Barrett-Lennard, 2010), even consulting (Tomaschek, 2006, p. 55).

That's what this book is all about – mutual contribution. And the experiment of having twelve authors write it tested this concept of "co-actualization" to the max. Did it succeed? Read the book, and I believe you'll agree – it succeeds with flying colors!

References

Goleman, D. (2000). Leadership that gets results. *Harvard Business Review, March/April,* 78-90.

Motschnig-Pitrik, R. (2008). Significant learning communities as environments for actualizing human potentials. *International Journal of Knowledge and Learning, 4 (4),* 387-397.

Motschnig-Pitrik, R., & Barrett-Lennard, G. (2010). Co-Actualization: A new construct in understanding well-functioning relationships. *Journal of Humanistic Psychology, 50 (3),* 374-398.

Ryback, D. (1989). An interview with Carl Rogers. *Person-Centered Review, 4 (1),* 99-112.

Tomaschek, N. (2006). *Systemic Coaching.* Heidelberg: Carl-Auer.

Preface

A most natural way to learn is learning from experience. We engage in it constantly. Whether we drive a car, ride our mountain bike, organize a party or give a presentation, doing it for the first time is hardest. It gets easier each time.

At this point you might be asking: But what does experiential learning have to do with this book? A book can support professional development, provide entertainment or serve some other purpose, but it doesn't allow gaining experience, or does it? At best, a professional book can support us in constructing knowledge that is relevant to some subject matter like project management. Alternatively, it can give guidelines on how to manage more successfully. But can a book provide experiential learning?

We, the team of authors, want you to find out. We want you to see in which ways this book can help you make deeper sense out of your experience. The book intends to provide you with a path that will help you to explore and gain understanding of your own experience. This path is paved with a multitude of experiences that we – an international team of a dozen practitioners and researchers – made by closely cooperating in a large project over a period of four years. The path starts with briefly revealing the backdrop of the journey, our basic assumptions and values, in order to let you orient yourself as to whether you want to join us on the journey. Next, the path leads through our experiential landscape by passing through several case-examples arranged by themes. But this guided tour through our experiential landscape is intended to be just the beginning of your journey. Its main part is going to be your own engagement, elaboration, and insight of referring back and forth to *your* own experience in a reflective circle. Towards the end of our journey, you will be sensitized to choose your own trails and invite your co-workers to join you. So you'll keep travelling along, gaining ever more experience or, in other words, learning experientially – which we believe is a deep and sustainable way of self-directed and collaborative learning.

Let us introduce ourselves as your companions on our journey: We, the iCom team, are a dozen information technology colleagues united by the fact that we cooperated on the International Constructive Communication (iCom) project (www.icomproject.eu). We all work at the interface between software engineering, ICT-project management, human resource development and continuing education. In our work, we aim to build bridges between industry and academia. We direct our research at practical issues. Foremost, we aim to improve ICT-related projects by taking into account a vast scope of issues ranging from interpersonal attitudes and communication to the specification of business processes and inclusion of end-users in all major decisions. In a nutshell, we feel we gained a lot of valuable experience that we don't want to keep just to ourselves.

When writing, we faced a conflict between being as authentic and open as possible and protecting information that colleagues might prefer not to share now with the whole world. The resolution we found was for some authors to directly self-disclose at times and obscure names and identifying information at other times. Thus, if you think you can identify a person or organization this may really be the case and was intended; yet you can't be sure so as to protect confidentiality throughout. We hope this compromise between publicity and privacy is a decent one even though we are aware it is not optimal. Based on our experience and reflection, we offer the following suggestions for maximum sustainable benefit:

- Read the book in pieces and allow yourself time to reflect.
- Enter the cases with an open mind. Try to figure out what each one means to you and whether you have experiences that support or contradict them.
- After reading a case, accept the invitations to reflect. Find your personal responses to the questions before reading our insights and ideas for handling the case.
- Read the book with a team. The short, accessible chapters make the book ideal for team development. Read a case per day, or week, and share your reactions with others.
- We're sure that you will come up with further ideas or will even protest against ours. We'd very much appreciate it if you shared your thoughts with us and our readers on the iCom website at www.icomproject.eu.

Gradually, you may enter a mode in which you come to kindly welcome and appreciate your own experience, whether pleasant or less so. In this way, you can identify your own issues for you and your team to reflect upon – and learn experientially and sustainably.

Enjoy your trip!

The iCom team,

Vienna and Brno in September 2013

Introduction

A book with a dozen authors – can that work? This is a valid question, and in fact we asked it ourselves at the outset of this book project. But since nobody forced us to write a book together and each of us liked the idea of engaging in a publication together, we gradually developed a shared vision about this form of passing on part of our valuable experiences. It reflects a significant part of our multi-faceted experience in collaborating together and with partners from industry, aided through and influenced by various electronic media along the way.

Adhering to our shared values and unfolding wisdom that formed throughout the years, the book process itself became one of agile and lean management and included the target audience from the project idea onward. Our communication and collaboration tended to unfold around a shared set of attitudes and values such as transparency, respect, and a desire to deeply understand the other person including their context from which the iCom project had been built. This, we believe made the process a democratic, constructive, and engaging one, even though not minimal in terms of the time resources we chose to invest. In any case, if you as the reader learn approximately as much as we did while putting the topics and cases together, the book will have served its purpose well.

At this point let us invite you to find out how this 12-author book can serve you and – regardless where you are now – inspire you to grow towards more effectiveness and satisfaction in your social and work contexts, noting that they are intricately intertwined. If you work in a field related to Information and Communication Technology (ICT), your work experience will be close to ours such that several example-cases will speak to you directly. If, however, your occupation is a different one, you may still find parallels and deviations and learn by establishing the connections between your practices and those reflected in this book. Regardless of your origin, we trust that our multi-author and multi-level perspective of ICT-project work will provide some fresh and inspirational resources for each reader who is open enough to receiving them, even though not each case may intrigue every reader equally intensively.

The remainder of this introduction is aimed at introducing both the subject matter and the structure of the handbook. For consistency, the structure of the rest of the introduction is similar to the structure of the chapters of the handbook. In the section called "topic" we put forward a major proposition and characterize it briefly. Then, a number of cases illustrate and illuminate the topic from various perspectives and provide resources for a follow up reflection and collection of ideas on how to handle similar situations. In order to provide some theoretical grounding and motivation to engage with the handbook, the introductory topic description is more detailed than the remaining topic characterizations.

Fostering constructive communication while gaining domain-specific competence

What we learned throughout our journey was that whether a project succeeds or fails, depends prominently on the project manager's and team's competencies as well as on their internal and external communication in any context. None of these factors comes free and all need volition, devotion, effort, and attuned peers to continuously improve them (Ryback, 1998). Regardless of whether you start high or low in competencies, thoughtful and reflective practice has the potential to advance every team and to contribute to their success, reduction of emotional strain, and increase in the qualities making up a "healthy" team.

The authors of this handbook engaged in a four-year long project of promoting constructive international communication in the context of ICT (iCom). Part of our endeavor consisted in finding out, what were the typical challenges in today's businesses and projects.

Organizations, such as companies, governmental institutions or Non-Governmental Organizations (NGOs), are socially complex and dynamic systems. An organizational system is more than the sum of its parts. When people come together and work for a company, a strategy or an idea to accomplish something, it's always for something more than one person can do. If people work together they create a "new world". This is because they communicate about their assumptions, their ideas and their perceptions of the world. And the fascinating thing from a constructivist point of view is, that if people speak and work together, they create a new view of the world (or of a problem, project, solution). This is the important starting point for any productive growing of anything: people have to communicate with each other. Only after realizing this, new things are able to arise.

It's like a good football team. Each member is very important. Everyone brings a lot of skills into the team. But a successful team is formed, when all parts of the team have a common idea of the "big picture" of their game. They need a consciousness about the "system". A football (or soccer) team, just like an organization, is a complex, dynamic system consisting of individuals who are differentiated by functions (e.g., trainer, fullback, forward) and structures (e.g., formation, plays). They generate collective behavioral patterns, which are based on system parameters. A successful organizational system "football team" is therefore highly correlated, motivated and aware of their common goals and collective abilities. Organizational awareness is therefore an important system parameter for a productive team.

A football match is characterized by its non-linear dynamic (just like the market situation of an enterprise). It is determined by phase transitions between game situations, which range from balance to shifts to chaos. In chaotic situations, the system is highly sensitive to the smallest incident, which may lead to deciding events (e.g., penalty, goal) and results ("butterfly effect[1]"). Consequently, the team spirit as collective system parameter could collapse. The momentum changes. Then, the players behave in an uncorrelated or unmotivated manner. That's the dynamic of organizations, a dynamic in all forms of organizational systems (companies, universities, municipalities, families, etc.).

Organization consists of human beings and their interactions. The challenge for companies is to place the right people in the right positions. Competencies and skills, like the situations in which we are operating, are continuously changing. Therefore, organizations have to be flexible to support employees and for employees to change their roles within the company (Schloemer & Tomaschek, 2010).

The second point is to think about "interactions". There is no organizational system without the interactions of individuals. That's the important thing. You can buy eleven superstar athletes, but this doesn't automatically make you win the champions league. You need a successful team, which communicates very effectively. Only then productivity, efficiency and innovation are possible.

If you really want an effective, productive and innovative organization you need some key factors of a transforming process for the organization:
- Develop employees' comprehensive understanding of the organization.
- Foster a desire to contribute to the organization's success.
- Resolve internal boundaries and obstacles throughout change processes.
- Enhance bottom-up change process ("Change process starts within oneself"), decentralization, and self-organization tendencies.
- Decrease powerlessness and increase a sense of inclusion or belonging so that everybody can contribute to the organization on a daily basis.
- Provide "leadership" that does not hinder, but rather supports innovation – communication without taboos but with respect toward each person.

---

1   This refers to how one butterfly's stroke of its wings then and there can lead to a tornado here and now.

- Create system parameters that facilitate self-organization (e.g., give employees the opportunity to take more responsibility; allow them to make more decisions; and decentralize decision-making to lessen central-hierarchical decision-making).

The perception of the organization as a large entity is a characteristic of an "Innovative Future Enterprise" and it's the foundation of each successful team and their communication. In effective teams you can see that everybody takes responsibility for the whole. Every team member is focusing on the goal, following a shared vision and is full of energy and spirit to work in the team. The team follows an intensive reciprocal learning method, communicates with unusual openness and is really living a concept of community with a positive view of the world. In these teams innovation is always possible! To us it tends to emerge almost "naturally" since creative ideas are welcomed, and processes to follow-up on the most promising ones are in place. Several cases in this book provide manifested examples and invite you to reflect on them and be touched by the innovative spirit. Innovative future enterprises are also characterized by new work styles enabling people to become more creative, flexible, self-organizing and innovative. Ask yourself the following questions to find out where your team is now on its path toward becoming an innovative future enterprise:
- How freely are things internally and externally communicated?
- Open innovation: How present is the customer in the organization?
- What is the role of "intuition": How much space does the organization provide for emotions, intuition, spontaneity and creativity?
- How is the work environment designed: Does the workplace support communication and innovative actions?
- How is the corporate culture defined: Do we attract the best employees (for the right jobs)?
- How intensively do we use technology and Social Media in our role as driving force for innovation?

Probably you'll agree that healthy, constructive interpersonal communication is vital to moving forward the organizational dimension. So let's look into this too. On the interpersonal level, our path was significantly influenced by a humanistic, person-centered mindset and approach. In a nutshell, the basic hypothesis underlying this approach is that communication tends to be forward directed or constructive, if all partners receive each other's transparency and openness, respect, and intent to understand each other. This style of interaction provides a complex way of being that includes subjective and emotional aspects. Let us explain this essential condition by a few examples and see how it extends to project management.

Transparency and *openness* stand on the opposite to obscurity, pretending, hiding, and distortion. A transparent, open partner does not necessarily mean to expose everything, like business secrets or strong, immediate emotions, but they do mean to expose trustingly and courageously as much as is appropriate to the situation at hand.

The open-source movement and open-access policies are good examples of this principle that shares and collaborates between individual units and transcends their borders or limits. Also transparent project goals, strategies, and communication paths can be seen as manifestations of the principle of openness. At a personal level at which the concept of openness had originally been specified (Rogers, 1959), a human being who is open to his or her experience and that of others will likely be able to learn from each situation and expand their mental images, flexibly welcoming and integrating new information. Such a person will have and express active interest in their surroundings (Barrett-Lennard, 2013) and furthermore be able to sense what is going on in themselves and be able to share it if deemed appropriate. For example, if a customer expressed his discomfort with a service a company was offering, an open employee would express their honest concern and tend to listen to the customer to find out as much as possible about the customer's source of complaint and dissatisfaction in order to be able to help fixing or transforming the problem. He/she might be aware of his disappointment or fear of the situation or its consequences, but he/she accepts those emotions rather than behave defensively, focusing instead upon the customer's concern and how to approach it to learn and change him- or herself, the situation, and his or her organization for the better.

In the example above, listening to the customer already communicates two further essential attitudes: *Respect* and making an effort to understand. *Respecting* or *accepting* the other person means to take them seriously and to accept their having their own views, feelings, meanings, opinions, and values that might well differ from ours. Respect, however, does not necessarily mean agreement, since this would contradict openness in the case that we see the world differently. Respect, however, means to meet the other at eye level of personhood, to opt for dialogue and participation rather than defensiveness, manipulation, or exerting power over the other, and to include rather than exclude them from one's thought and action. In the example mentioned, listening to the customer would not result in telling him/

her what *he/she* is misunderstanding or doing wrong, but in encountering the problem together as partners with mutual trust to solve it as best as is possible under the given circumstances.

But respecting the other is not enough unless we also try to *understand* him or her thoroughly in their context and subject matter. This third capacity and skill is strongly related to empathic understanding (Rogers, 1961) and encompasses thorough listening to all aspects of the other's message including his/her tone of voice, body language, gesticulation, words, meanings, context, looks, and factual context in order to receive a complex message, emotionally as well as intellectually/logically. This message is decoded in the given context with as much openness to all its aspects as we can afford. This process may result in checking our understanding with the customer, such as: "If I got you right, the system becomes very slow at peak access times and your employees resent this a lot?" or asking the customer deepening questions, such as: "Can you tell me which queries exactly lead to unacceptably long response times?" As a simple heuristic, the conversation will be directed toward thoroughly understanding the other person. Typically, it will be void of premature interrupting, criticizing, putting down or blaming the other person which all might signal lack of openness and/or respect.

It is essential that for constructive communication, the set of interdependent capacities described above be internalized or held by one person or preferably all partners at least to some degree. Thus, once one person would have listened to another that other person would listen with openness and respect in turn. But what can we do if the other, in our perception, lacks these capacities? Frequently, respectful listening and sharing engenders reciprocity. It can amaze team members to see how if they are not defensive and listen respectfully, the other person will magically begin to help them solve the situation at hand with a respectful response back. In our experience it is worth trying to live and provide openness, respect, and the intent to understand to a high degree. The other person will likely catch and imitate since these attitudes and capacities are contagious. Unfortunately, facilitative interactive styles are hard to be "taught" in a conventional sense and need to be modeled and perceived from other persons to become manifest in one's behavior, personality, and organization (Cornelius-White & Harbaugh, 2010).

Thus, strongly simplified, the ever unfolding "manifesto" or deeply ingrained "agenda" of constructive communication can be summarized as follows:

Mutual openness and transparency	rather than	obscurity, pretending, hiding, distortion
Mutual respect and acceptance	rather than	exclusion, looking down, putting down, blaming
Mutual encompassing, complex understanding	rather than	ignorance, misunderstanding, manipulating, rejecting
Interconnectedness, interdependence, and flow	rather than	fragmentation, dependence, imposed control, and rigidity

Table 1: Interwoven aspects of an "inner agenda" of constructive communication (adapted from Motschnig and Nykl (2014)

Intriguingly, the "inner agenda" can nicely be utilized when reflecting on problems. We bet that when you encounter a problem (that is not purely intellectual or "material"), at least one of the capacities described above will be lacking, usually in both/all parties. The cases in the handbook, amongst your own ones, will provide you with an ample sample for testing your opinions and forming wisdom.

You may also want to use the above Table 1 to ask and assess yourself where in this continuum you would place yourself or individual members of your team, or even the team as a whole. Time, will, and team-climate permitting, you could ask your team members to evaluate themselves, you, the team, other members, and then compare the results, reflect on them and formulate a shared vision as to common goals. We trust you use your and your team's creativity to invent other uses of the Table 1, such as to ask customers or friends and compare reflect, imagine, and so on, and perhaps even get back to the iCom team as we are intrigued by attempts to directly assess and improve facilitative communication.

The experienced reader will realize that besides interpersonal qualities like openness, acceptance and understanding, organizational conditions can allow or block co-workers and managers to implement the constructive communication "agenda" to a meaningful degree. In fact, the final item "interconnectedness, interdependence, and flow" – still calling for explanation – is recursive, being both an enabling condition of the first three aspects, and a bridge to wider scope and reach. Let us elaborate on this enabling and bridging aspect a bit.

How could I be open, if the organizational hierarchy doesn't allow me to talk to my boss other than in a few formal meetings with a fixed schedule? How can I effectively be open to a customer's justified suggestion if a too rigid project plan hinders me to take it into account? How can I utilize a bright, innovative idea that just unfolded in the team's dialogue (based on openness, respect and understanding that gave rise to a flow and forming of ideas), if the next obligatory deliverable forces me to stick to the production plan and deliver a tool that is outdated from the current perspective?

Examples such as these indicate that first, constructive communication needs interconnectedness and a permissive rather than rigidly controlled climate to unfold in organizations and projects. Secondly, the examples illustrate that open and respectful communication is particularly essential in agile (or lean) approaches to management. This is because, highly interconnected structures and open, constructive communication can be utilized to reciprocally support a constructive flow between persons, partners and adaptable artifacts rather than viewing artifacts as ultimate dogmas and building rigid walls that block the natural free flow between subsystems.

In order to make this topic self-contained we invite the reader to a brief excursion into agile management. The good fit of constructive communication and agile management comes from the fact that agile methods (for management and software development) not only take flow and hence the need for change into account (Beck et al., 2001), they fundamentally count on it. Agile methods are in tune with modern, more democratic management styles that favor team- and customer participation (Highsmith, 2004; Senge, 2006) and they thrive on interaction and fast feedback cycles to increase the probability of the "final" product meeting the customer's needs. Naturally, adapting continuously to the changing environment is an advantage in business as it has been in the evolution of species and cultural and legal systems (Damasio, 2012).

In the last decade, agile methods have come to be appreciated in a variety of fields (Highsmith, 2004). One prominent example is software development. In that field the authors of the *"Manifesto for Agile Software Development"* (Beck et al., 2001) could improve the ways of developing software by adopting the following value *preferences*, although not completely discarding the "traditional" values. They value:

- Individuals and interactions over processes and tools,
- Working software over comprehensive documentation,
- Customer collaboration over contract negotiation, and
- Responding to change over following a plan.

Interestingly, these value preferences show a clear shift towards the human being in collaborative relationship with fellow human beings – be it a team member or a customer – and away from "design constructs" like contracts, plans, tools and documentations. This may be the response to traditional methods' overemphasis on the artificial constructs and a perceived missing satisfaction of the human "players" in such an environment. These issues will be illustrated, in particular, by specific cases of the topic: *"Hold constructs flexibly"*.

After having returned from the excursion to agile methods, let us follow a few real cases that illustrate how the principles underlying this topic ("Foster constructive communication while gaining domain-specific competence") were manifested in the construction of this experience-based guide. Retrospectively, we see it as a small but revealing and highly experiential subproject of the overall iCom project.

Constructive communication while gaining domain-specific competence   27

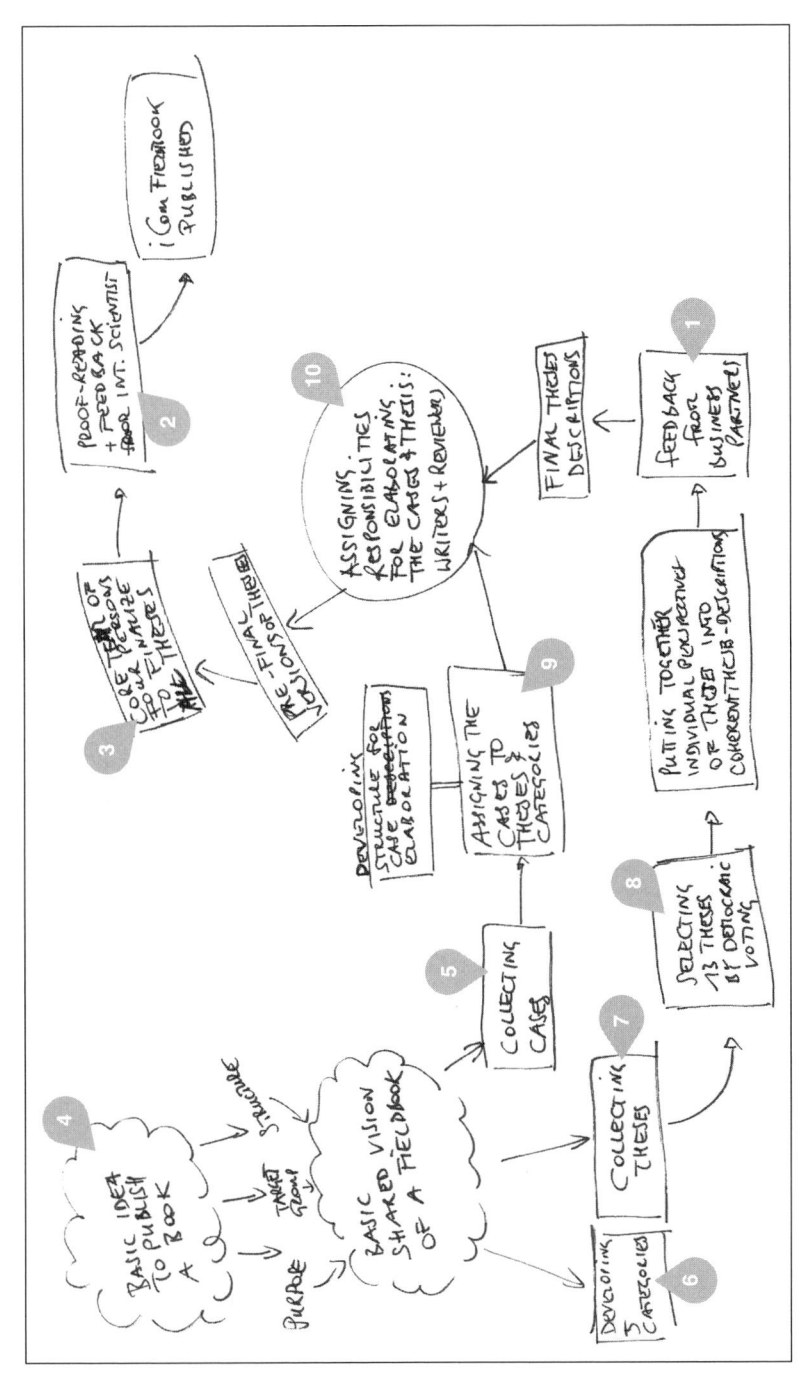

Figure 1: Book Development Process Model

We thought the best way to introduce our book was to use the case format that is a signature element. We provide two cases that present the agile, collaborative process that is a central theme of not only the content of the book, but also the process by which it was built, including the challenges of building a truly shared vision with many challenges.

Case 1:
The agile, collaborative process of the iCom book

Keywords: Agile management, agile process, end-user inclusion, flexibility, collaboration.

Situation
One of the cases of this book elaborates on the fact that agile and lean strategies aren't only relevant to software development but rather reach far beyond the production of software. Can they also be useful for writing a book?

Scenario
From the beginning of the book project we were clear about the primary audience: Managers from the field of Information and Communications Technology (ICT) and all those who'd like to improve their communication in the context of teamwork. So, basically, we would see them as our "end-users" or clients/customers. Being convinced about the vital importance of including them early, we planned various loops with including business partners but also other colleagues from ICT-management. Figure 1 illustrates the full process of book development using a flow chart and pins that will be explained throughout this chapter.

Essentially, we engaged business partners in various formal and informal ways:
- Invited them to author or co-author cases,
- Asked them to publish their statements that we had collected during project-events,
- Talked to them about the book or parts thereof in informal meetings, and

- Included two formal feedback loops in the early process of the iCom book (see Figure 1 the "Book development process model" on page 27, pin 1 in the bottom right corner).

To begin, we asked five business colleagues to give us feedback on the short descriptions of each of the 13 topics of the book that we sent out to them. We wanted to know whether the messages of the topics spoke to them. Later, we sent a fully elaborated topic (*"The team is the most wonderful place to learn"*) for feedback asking whether, in their view, managers would like to read a book that was structured in a way to include more chapters akin to the one we sent to them.

In general, we were encouraged to hear that the structure and short cases were perceived as convenient to read, thought provoking, and even fun for people who didn't have much time for reading long books. Moreover, the practitioners liked the technical topics better than some of us expected. This certainly provided valuable information and influenced the selection, elaboration and the omission of cases that were already written! Finally, after the manuscript was almost complete, two colleagues from the iCom team who had business experience read it and made final adaptations. Highly valuable comments, questions and ideas on finishing up the topics came from our American colleague Jef who also had acted as a consultant in the iCom project. While his primary responsibility was linguistic editing, he enriched the book with deepening inputs and made us alert to all the things that we didn't see anymore (see Figure 1, pin 2).

We planned a clear timeline and scope of the book, and designed its basic structure quite early in the project. However, to manage effectively the evolving issues that inevitably rise, we formed a small team of four delegates, two from the Brno sub-team and two from the Vienna-based sub-team (see Figure 1, pin 3). We worked in a coordinated, but basically self-organizing team where each of us had an influence on the process and its outcome. Consultation with end-users (our target audience) was in part planned in advance and in part happened spontaneously as we had a genuine interest to produce a book that would "speak" to project managers and team members. Who could give us better feedback?

Comment

It should also be said that not all colleagues from the team agreed to have the formal feedback loops since they cost time and effort and not everybody was convinced that a small number of respondents would be sufficient for our purpose. Hence, in some sense we were lucky that the respondents frequently agreed, otherwise we'd have to have significantly adapted our procedures and plans. The book-process provided innumerable opportunities to learn what it means to experience an agile process and to live in a quite self-organizing team that works on their product, in our case a book having an innovative, case-based format that is inherently transdisciplinary.

> **Invitation to reflect**
> - Do you think it makes sense to get feedback in an early phase from a small number of representatives of the target group only?
> - When, for you, would be the right time to include end-users when producing an innovative product?
> - Do you have ideas other than those mentioned above on employing agile strategies in producing documents?

Insights

Some issues are best to be specified early while others are better considered when they actually occur and become relevant.

Agile processes require openness and time for feedback loops.

Listening to others' views bears a vast potential for learning and creating a better product.

Potential strategies

Start early to include end-users so good ideas get a chance to be shared and can crystallize. In contrast, if time is so tight to include them later, feedback may not get a chance to be considered.

Be true to your vision but also believe in nature's law of ideas unfolding in the flow of events and be mindful of new revelations.

Case 2:
Building a shared vision of the iCom book-project

Keywords: Shared vision, dialogue, sensing.

Situation

One of the planned iCom project outcomes was a book resulting from our insights. In the final project year it became increasingly clear that the iCom book would draw on our practical experiences emanating from the project context itself. The scenario below illustrates our effort to build a shared vision. In particular it describes how we met two major challenges expressed in the following questions:

- What if one (responsible) party already worked on a common piece (here the book idea and basic structure) in advance? How do we integrate the other at a later point and still have them included as equal partners?
- How do we refine the book idea and agree on the contents and writing assignments in a distributed team of twelve persons who all want to contribute?

Elaborating a shared vision of a non-trivial project is not easy, even for a team of experienced researchers. Writing a book with 12 collaborators might normally lead to a strategy where the work is simply divided into an appropriate number of individual chapters and the responsibility is left to individual authors. But this is not what we wanted. We aimed at putting our ideas together. We wanted to illustrate how our shared experiences had "multi-faceted truths" and took divergent paths toward a common resolution that we wanted to share with our readers. So, how did we go about this?

Scenario

Both the Brno and Vienna sub-teams knew that the iCom book was one of the scheduled project deliverables. The University of Vienna, as the officially responsible partner, was expected to coordinate the book project, elaborate an initial proposal and then get the other partner "on board".

In Vienna we thought and spoke about the scope, audience, and structure of the book for quite some time before we actually scheduled a meeting to share our ideas on this topic (see Figure 1, pin 4). In this initial meeting it crystallized that we would write primarily for ICT-managers, that the core of the book would be short "stories" or cases that illustrate that "nothing works without appropriate communication and rarely does anything work better if people don't talk to each other." Also, an imagination was expressed as part of our vision: "While waiting for his/her plane at the airport, a manager would go the bookstore and find our book, open it, and immediately get caught by something that meets their interest – buy the book – and explore all the way until called to board the aircraft." While we didn't know exactly how we'd go about achieving these qualities, each of us went home with a shared imagination of the gross goal and with a considerable amount of creative tension on how we could achieve this goal together. We agreed to collect keywords pointing to issues we wanted to communicate to our readers as a next step. Also, we felt we'd need one person to overlook the whole complexity inherent in the genesis of the book. Thankfully, David agreed to take on the job of facilitating the book development process.

The next time we met we listened to each other's ideas and proposals regarding the content and the structure. We had come up with complementary ideas and put them together on a flipchart (Figure 2).

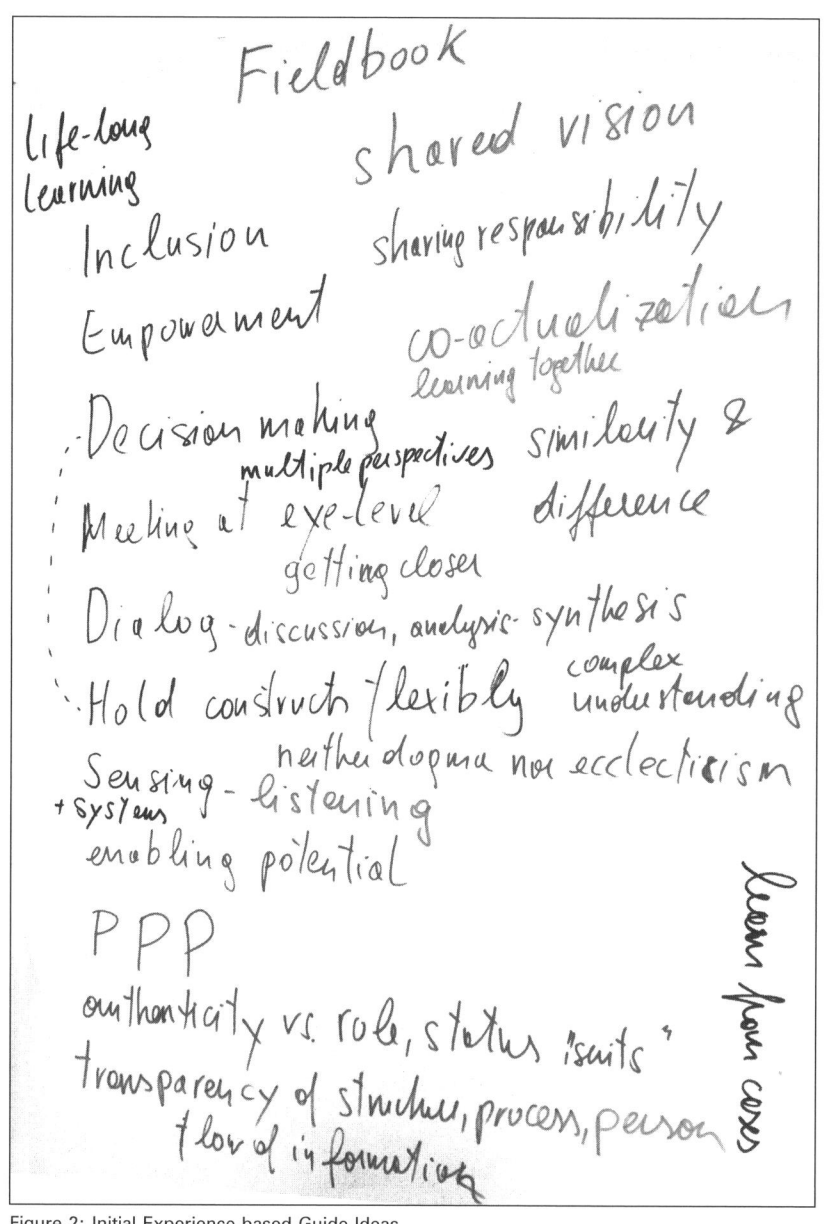

Figure 2: Initial Experience-based Guide Ideas

(handwritten fieldbook notes:)

Fieldbook
Life-long learning
Inclusion   shared vision
           sharing responsibility
Empowerment
           co-actualization
           learning together
Decision making
       multiple perspectives   similarity & difference
Meeting at eye-level
           getting closer
Dialog - discussion, analysis- synthesis
Hold constructs flexibly   complex understanding
         neither dogma nor ecclecticism
Sensing - listening
+ systems
enabling potential
PPP
authenticity vs. role, status "suits"
transparency of structure, process, person
   flow of information

learn from cases

In that meeting, the gross structure of case description crystallized. Central was the wish to associate each case somehow with calls for readers' reflections and "next steps to competencies" such as to motivate active engagement. We then collected cases from the project context (see Figure 1, pin 5). They would stem from the project documentation, personal memories or discussion with colleagues and business partners. But how would we coordinate the task? Spontaneously the idea arose to do it on the web, namely to create a spreadsheet for a systematic case collection and tagging of each case with the keywords we had collected during the meeting.

Then, Christina suggested five categories, like knowledge transfer, leadership, or communication, to which the cases could be assigned to create more structure (see Figure 1, pin 6). Besides this coarse structure we still aimed at finding an intermediate level that would capture the meaning of our keywords in such a way that it would get the attention of our target audience. Thus we also set out to search and collect in another spreadsheet "catch phrases" to reveal the keywords' meanings in an evocative, telling, and easily accessible fashion (see Figure 1, pin 7). Some of us met informally to check the understandings of some catch phrases and compare what they meant to each of us. At about that time, Renate (from the Vienna sub-team) talked to Tom (from the Brno sub-team) about the progress of the book and also openly shared her worries about how we could make the book project something really shared if we produced the core ideas in the Austrian sub-team and whether the colleagues in Brno would concur at all? Tom offered to talk to the Brno team about the book progress. He asked for any written documents and we scheduled a day when he would join the sub-team in Vienna *before* our major team-meeting on the iCom book would take place.

The next meeting of the Vienna sub-team in which Tom (from Brno) participated, was intriguing and quite effective, even though we had conflicting opinions about if, when, and how many of our business partners to include for early feedback and what exactly to ask them to comment on. Dissenting opinions were expressed and listened to. Nevertheless, we agreed to include business partners early in the process, consistent with an agile approach, one in which end-users (here readers) would be included in all stages of the process. We were really glad that Tom could join us in the next task, namely in deciding which of the 60 or so catch phrases we'd include and which ones to discard in the first run (see Figure 1, pin 8). Ad hoc we found a democratic procedure on how to select catch phrases, namely through voting. We went through each of the catch phrases, shared our feeling and meanings, and voted if it should be selected. Finally about 15 catch phrases remained and we eliminated 2 of them due to their similarity with other ones. Tom went back to Brno well informed about the status of the book and our shared thinking that he could pass on to the Brno sub-team.

About two months after the Vienna sub-team had started working on the iCom book, a meeting with all colleagues from Brno took place. While committed to building a shared vision, the participants in the sub-team from Vienna agreed that they would like to transparently state the following issues:
- A guided tour to: Where are we now in the process? What is still open and needs elaboration? And what matters a lot to us and should be kept?
- A proposal on how the sub-team in Vienna can imagine to proceed on the book with intensive collaboration with the colleagues in Brno. This proposal was presented as our perspective that definitely was nothing fixed but open to debate. The proposal included three options of involvement: Colleagues from Brno would:
  a) Help us elaborate those cases in which events and people from the Czech Republic were the major players by reviewing and adding to cases authored by the Vienna sub-team.
  b) Supply their own cases.
  c) A combination of a) and b).

Interestingly, there was a clear preference for option c). However, further sharing made it clear that the catch phrases – pointing to core themes – we had identified so far wouldn't cover some of the cases that colleagues from Brno wanted to contribute. So what should we do about it? After some clarifying dialogue that clearly communicated some different foci between the sub-teams that "naturally" existed in our work, we agreed that more technical cases would be added to the online case collection. In a subsequent meeting in Brno we would allocate cases to catch phrases and assign responsibilities for the further process of writing and reviewing thematic parts of the book (see Figure 1, pin 9).

The feeling that we succeeded in holding a shared vision was confirmed in the next team meeting in Brno. Bara nicely prepared cards with themes according to old and new catch phrases and produced colored cards for each case. We stood around a big table and collectively allocated cases to themes and shifted the cases so long as everybody seemed happy or exhausted enough to agree with this initial allocation (Figure 3).

Figure 3: Assigning cases to topics and categories

Then, each person chose a theme to be responsible for and one to review, such that we could work on actually writing the cases for the topics in a distributed, though not independent way (see Figure 1, pin 10): We all were interdependent on each other's inputs and comments, however the structure was clear and so were communication paths and media such that we could move on interdependently. We were destined to each put together "his or her" topics in a time frame of two months. Would we accomplish this shared goal?

In fact, the web space we had allocated for collecting the topics was filled by the end of the two months and hundreds of mails were passed between us with a comparable number of accesses to the shared online space. In brief, the major goal and steps to building our shared vision was accomplished. Technology was a big help in this process, indeed. We were clear though that lots of work was still ahead of us but it would build on a solid basis integrating our experiences, our work, and our insights according to ideas we had co-created.

Comment
Even though being quite complex already, the description above forms abstractions from other aspects of the shared vision like graphics, dealing with industry feedback, choice of publisher, etc.

Invitation to reflect
- What, in your view, contributed to arriving at a shared vision and going for it?
- Where do you see major challenges and risks in the process?
- Do you believe that the book vision is truly a shared one or could a truly shared vision be achieved only if all players started building it from the beginning?
- Can you identify and describe risks that remained once it was agreed that new themes might be added?
- Do you agree that the process of building a shared vision doesn't stop in an early project phase but continues throughout? If you agree, try to identify a few implications. If you disagree, explain why building a shared vision can stop at an early phase.

Insights

To build a shared vision, dialogue, a high degree of transparency and honesty, and sufficient openness to the ideas of others seem all to be essential conditions.

Including another party at a later point in time requires special thought, sensitivity and skill. It tends not to be easy but apparently can be done, although usually with some compromise on both sides!

Face-to-face meetings are indispensable for putting ideas together such that everybody has a consonant sense of the whole new construct.

New media are indispensable when collaborating in distributed teams and even putting artifacts like pieces of text together that are produced separately.

> **Renate:**
> Encounter tends to lead to multifaceted, complex understanding. Ignorance can be costly!
> Building a shared vision needs time and effort and it tends to result in an outcome that resides on some higher level since it better meets the needs of a larger amount of addresses.

> **David:**
> Respect goes along with patience. Know your viewpoint, however beware of premature judgment.

> **Christina:**
> If 100 people are working in your company and everybody has one idea how to enhance the company's success you have 100 valuable ideas without much effort. In very hierarchical company structures it is, in general, quite hard as a normal worker to have your idea reaching the management board, as several hierarchies might hinder that. Try to hold structures lean or encourage sharing ideas across hierarchical boundaries (e.g., through a company-internal voluntarily competition).

> **Tom:**
> A truly shared vision is not only agreed but also really elaborated together.

Potential strategies

When aiming for a truly shared vision, include partners as soon as possible.

Alternate between face-to-face meetings and online phases thoughtfully.

Agree on a strategy and file structure when using online media.

When cooperating closely with colleagues, risk to be as transparent as possible *and* listen to the other as mindfully as you manage.

Our insights

Reflecting what we learned while applying an agile process and aiming to communicate constructively in our team can be summarized as follows: Agile processes require instant and effective communication and decision-making. They tend to bring people together and keep them engaged to reach the common goals. In complex situations it seems sheer impossible to determine everything in advance and just follow a rigid workflow.

When used thoughtfully and skillfully, new media can improve the team's effectiveness. This may be due to the fact that some tasks are better accomplished individually while others benefit from multiple perspectives, team-thinking and collaboration.

It may be hard and require considerable effort to convince team members of a "shared vision" if they don't participate in its inception or "birth".

Next steps to competencies

Organizations, teams, and individuals can take steps to becoming more competent in communicating constructively to best work on the tasks at hand.

Do some of the following ideas make sense to you?

- Organization
  - Create, revisit and potentially upgrade the organization's vision at appropriate times, in particular, if new employees join the organization or changes become beneficial.
  - Find ways to listen to your employee's and customer's visions. Encourage them to form and express their vision openly.

- Team
  - Get to know your team members and their interests, strengths and weaknesses. Think and try to find out how you can complement each other best. Share openly yet respectfully.
  - Read the iCom book in small parts and reflect on them in the team.
  - Use the materials on our website: www.icomproject.eu

- Individual
    - Allocate some time to devote to the book. Even better: Find colleagues/friends who will do the same so you can reflect together.
    - Add to the cases of individual topics (and share them with the iCom team). You'll realize that when you write down your experiences you'll gain insight by the mere fact of putting your thoughts, feelings and meanings into words!

Final reflections

In what ways do you agree with these statements?
Everything can be said; it depends mostly on *how* it is said.

"Experience is, for me, the highest authority. The touchstone of validity is my own experience."
Carl Rogers (1961, p. 23)

Two heads are better than one. Twelve heads are better than two.

References

Barrett-Lennard, G. T. (2013). *The relationship paradigm. Human Being Beyond Individualism*. UK: Palgrave McMillan.
Beck, K., Beedle, M., van Bennekum, M., Cockburn, A., Cunningham, W., Fowler, M., Grennings, J., Highsmith, J., Hunt, A., Jeffries, R., Kern, J., Marick, B., Martin, R. C., Mellor, S., Schwaber, K., Sutherland, J., & Thomas, D. (2001). *The agile manifesto*. In: *Agile Alliance*. http://www.agilealliance.org/the-alliance/the-agile-manifesto/ (retrieved on 30/9/2013).
Cornelius-White, J. H., & Harbaugh, A. P. (2010*). Learner-centered instruction: Building relationships for student success*. Thousand Oaks, CA: Sage Publications.
Damasio, A. R. (2012). *The Self Comes to Mind*. London: Vintage.
Highsmith, J. (2004). *Agile Project Management: Creating Innovative Products*. Boston, USA: Pearson Education.
Motschnig, R., & Nykl, L. (2014). *Person-centred communication: Theory, Skills, and Practice*. London: McGraw Hill. (German original in 2009 by Klett-Cotta; Czech translation in 2011 by Grada).

Rogers, C. R. (1959). A Theory of Therapy, Personality, and Interpersonal Relationships, as Developed in the Client-Centered Framework. In: *Psychology: A Study of a Science*. Vol. 3, S. Koch, ed., New York, Toronto, London: McGraw Hill, Inc.

Rogers, C. R. (1961). *On Becoming A Person – A Psychotherapists' View of Psychotherapy*. London: Constable.

Ryback, D. (1998). *Putting Emotional Intelligence to Work*. Boston, USA: Butterworth-Heinemann.

Schloemer, S., & Tomaschek, N. (2010). *Leading in Complexity. New Ways of Management*. Heidelberg: Carl-Auer Verlag.

Senge, P. M. (2006). *The Fifth Discipline, The Art & Practice of the Learning Organization*. New York, USA: Currency Doubleday.

Knowledge Transfer

Connect the dots

No man is an island. **We all live in a world that is highly interconnected. In particular, human beings need relationships to survive.** The necessity of social connection is evident and can be observed, for example, in the boom of web-based social networks. **In that sense, every person can be regarded as an independent dot, while at the same time being interconnected with others.** For a whole system (a team, an organization or society in general), the structure and its quality will depend not primarily on the dots in particular but on the arcs interconnecting them.

Relations and interactions with others enable us to gain new insights and expand our horizon. **In a complex work context, such as an international ICT (Information and Communication Technology) project team, exploring and connecting different sides of the project situation can bring new opportunities to light that otherwise might have remained undiscovered.** For organizations it is not only internal relationships that help to create innovative ideas and solutions. Interdisciplinarity and diversity of work contexts within and between organizations can be highly beneficial for work groups. Why not invite a colleague from outside and listen to his/her reactions? Almost inevitably you'll inspire each other and create new connections.

As humans we have to accept our natural boundaries – we simply cannot know everything. The challenge is to know where we can find information and whom we have to connect with. Information itself is not necessarily of value. It is essential to understand it in a certain context, to connect it to previous experiences and find ways to make use of it. In other words:

We need to be able to connect different people and different pieces of information to create meaning out of them.

How can managers benefit from connecting the dots? Essential questions to be asked are:
- What are high quality connections and under what conditions do they develop?
- What can I do to promote high quality connections?
- What could destroy high quality connections?

Keywords: Lifelong learning, systems sensing, networking, multiple perspectives, manager-teacher interaction, learning from cases, innovation, unlearning, distributed teams, communication channels, new media, media-choice.

Cases

Overview of cases

- Case 1 captures some of the managers' insights when **"Connecting science and business"** in iCom Practice-Research Workshops.

- Case 2 **"ICT-Managers inspire innovative computer-science education"** describes how a teacher got inspired by ICT-Managers to innovate his computer-science education at school to make it more authentic and motivating for his pupils.

- Case 3 **"Re-education and unlearning needed?"** confirms that such innovations are in fact necessary, if *"re-education and unlearning"* on the job shall be prevented.

- The final Case 4 reveals some practical experiences around the ubiquitous theme of **"Connecting in distributed teams"** and provides some hints on choosing communication media deliberately and creatively.

Case 1:
Connecting science and business

Keywords: Practice-Research Workshop, university-industry collaboration, researching business practice, multiple perspectives, innovation.

Situation

Within the iCom project we organized a series of "Practice-Research Workshops" which aimed at connecting students, researchers and practitioners working in various positions in the ICT-sector. In this context, "connecting the dots" meant bringing people together who we thought would be able to learn from each other and develop new perspectives. We offered them a space for exchanging experiences and knowledge, for discussing issues that commonly arise in many businesses in the ICT-sector and provided students with the opportunity to gain a better understanding of practice-related work processes and current developments in the market. Students and researchers joined the small group discussions and, in turn, gave research-based feedback to the business partners. Besides presentations of research and speeches from practitioners, a large part of the workshops was devoted to problem-based small group discussions that were facilitated through the project team. For the small group discussions, the business partners could bring in their own authentic cases from their organization. Receiving feedback from multiple sources helped them to reflect upon their cases and look at them from new angles. While some participants only took part in a few selected workshops, there were others who were regularly involved and became part of the iCom network, meaning there was more exchange with students, also outside the workshops.

Scenario

There were several regular participants. One of the regular participants was a project manager from "Kentico Software", an international software company based in Brno, Czech Republic. Trying to explore the real benefits of the workshops for our business partners, we interviewed the participant about his personal experiences with iCom. His feedback shows the importance of interpersonal factors in university-industry collaboration.

iCom: iCom team member   *A:* Antonín M. from Kentico company

iCom: "How did you hear about the iCom-workshops?"

A: "The head of Kentico and a professor from the Czech part of the iCom team knew each other from university, so I got in contact with the professor and he invited me to join the workshop. The topics were really interesting, and I appreciated that the other participants wanted to learn from my experiences at Kentico. From the first contact I was persuaded that the iCom team really wanted to support business partners to change something in practice. The PhD-students asked questions that I found to be very interesting and close to my job."

iCom: "In which ways did you find the workshops inspiring for your work?"

A: "I regularly meet with colleagues, but I found the exchange with researchers and PhD-students to be very fruitful as they have other perspectives that are in many ways also very practice-related. From the last iCom activity that I attended in Brno I learned about personal visions. This is something that I used last week in a workshop where we prepared a vision for the whole company from the process point of view. The experience from iCom helped me to start the workshop and see if everyone was going the same way and then they developed a strong vision."

iCom: "Can you remember any significant experiences from the workshops?"

A: "I remember when I met the scientific head of the project from the Austrian side of the iCom team. I felt that she really understood what I told her about current issues in our company and without really knowing the context; she immediately knew what I meant. Right there I realized that this was not only my point of view but also that other people had a similar perspective on it. This helped me to better understand the issue."

Another regular participant of the Practice-Research-Workshops was Marcello, a software-developer who runs his own business. He is also a PhD-student at the Faculty of Computer Science of the University of Vienna. For him, the main driving force for attending the workshops were potential synergies between theory and practice that could support his research work. During the workshop sessions that he attended, he noticed that practitioners would often follow rather simple approaches to find quick solutions while researchers would elaborate the cases in more detail. His learning experiences from the workshops were mainly connected to his business practices. The workshops helped him to change perspectives in complex situations (to switch from a practice-related viewpoint to a research-oriented viewpoint) and to pay more attention to the general business environment. Yet another participant, a computer scientist and independent consultant, stated: "What I liked best was the 'iCom Format': A great deal of interaction instead of frontal lectures. Practice and science interweaved seamlessly – different cultures encountering each other. In brief: Rich diversity and little mono-chronicity in a dynamic and friendly welcoming atmosphere. One thing you need to take care of is that the small team moderators don't get distracted by other tasks. They are important to keep the conversation on track."

Comment

The Practice-Research Workshops did not aim at providing recipes for dealing with issues or managing projects. Rather, they wanted to inspire both students and practitioners to problem solve and help them reflect their own situations and practices by getting in contact with others.

Invitation to reflect
- Who are your sparring partners, with whom do you exchange experiences?
- What fields are they from and why is their perspective especially valuable to you?
- Think about a recent issue in your work context that really bothered you. Who did you talk to about the issue? Was their input/feedback helpful?
- Think of someone you know who is not a practitioner in the field of ICT – what would this person say about the issue? Might this person be able to help you to see "the whole picture"?
- Try to capture the essence of the issue by explaining it in only three sentences to someone who isn't familiar with your work context.

Insights

A lot of project managers are involved in ICT-networks that provide them with news about current developments and insights into new technologies. Few networks are really interdisciplinary though, involving persons with different backgrounds and bridging the gaps between students and practitioners. The experiences from iCom participants show that this exchange tends to be highly valuable for both sides.

Potential strategies

Talking to the same colleagues about your work issues may not get you out of your comfort zone. Connecting with people from other contexts and backgrounds can help you to gain new perspectives, connect the dots, and see the whole picture.

Case 2:
ICT-Managers inspire innovative computer-science education

Keywords: Computer science education, ICT-companies, motivation, agile methods, coding, teamwork, school-industry collaboration.

Situation

Frequently, students at school can barely motivate themselves to learn or they see no reason why they should explore new things. It is not unusual that students learn purely for the purpose of successfully finishing the school year. One of the reasons is that students have little perspective of their personal development from what they learn at school. At the beginning of a school year students ask rather "What will I have to do for a positive grade?" instead of "What will I learn this school year?". This results in learning for school and learning for exams instead of learning for oneself. The point for the teacher is to provide students with perspectives so they can develop more motivation in what they learn. When students experience new learned things in computer-science as up-to-date topics of real ICT-companies, as for instance the agile approach, they realize that what they can learn at school is highly relevant for their future life as well. The following scenario illustrates how lifelong learning motivation in students can be established by providing them with perspectives from ICT-companies.

Scenario
During the Practice-Research Workshop in Chvalovice, teachers from Austria and the Czech Republic met with managers from ICT-companies. The surrounding vineyards provided a relaxing atmosphere and an ideal setting for informal talks between the participants. The focus was on how both sides, school and business world, could benefit from each other. Computer science teachers reported that students don't like to learn how to code computer programs as it seems to be hard work, similar to learning a new language.

On the other side, some of the ICT-managers reported that it is still important to learn how to create computer programs, but it is even more important to establish a beneficial, positive team atmosphere in a team of programmers. The workshop included a presentation on "Agile Methods in Organizing ICT-teams," and afterwards the idea emerged that such an approach could potentially work also in computer science lessons at school. We discussed how the approach might have a positive impact on students' motivation as they could learn to code within a cooperative climate.

The small workshop group of teachers and managers finally agreed that they will give this a try and planned some procedures. Some teachers tried to implement agile approaches in their coding classes while providing students the perspective that this way of work organization is common in ICT-companies, and the way they organize their learning is very similar to that. Subsequent research conducted by one of the teachers confirmed that students tend to be more motivated to learn how to code and cooperate better in teams.

Comment
During the Practice-Research Workshops teachers were usually involved to establish contacts with each other and with partners of ICT-companies. It turned out that especially ICT-managers were very interested in computer science education at school to discover and perhaps influence what students learn as preparation for their work life.

> **Invitation to reflect**
> - Do you know a school near you where they teach how to code?
> - Have you ever thought about to get in touch with this school?
> - Can you imagine organizing some informal cooperation for sharing ideas, plans and procedures for a project? Do you have an idea how your company and this school could benefit somehow from such cooperation as it was described in this case?
> - Can you imagine other forms of contact with students and consequent benefits for both sides? Is there a way you want to tap the creativity inherent in young people?

Insights

This example shows that involving schools and educational institutions in the iCom project and connecting them with ICT-companies can result in positive outcomes for both sides. The schools benefit with experienced up-to-date teachers and motivated students and the ICT-companies with better-prepared candidates of possible future colleagues.

Agile methods with their rich interactions and flexibility contribute to increasing motivation not only in ICT-developers and programmers but also in students.

Students like to be in touch with real problems and tend to release unknown resources when solving authentic problems.

Potential strategies

Higher motivation of pupils could be achieved if real ICT-managers visit a computer science lesson at school and explain to students how their projects are organized and conducted.

If more students get excited for ICT and learn already at school how teamwork is organized, companies can benefit by getting a better qualified work force.

Case 3:
Re-education and unlearning needed?

Keywords: Education, unlearning, soft skills, self-organization, school.

Situation
During an early iCom workshop, participants discussed the inadequacy of academic education of computer science students in the context of preparing them for their future jobs.

Scenario
T: (iCom team member)   *M1:* (Manager 1 from industry)
M2: (Manager 2 from industry)

T: "What do you think: should students come better equipped with soft skills or should the academic focus remain on conveying information and basic concepts?"

M1: "It depends on the instructor and his/her competencies. Usually, academic teachers are best in explaining computer science concepts, and understanding them is essential. At the same time, of course, better soft skills are needed! If the university doesn't manage to offer that, we need to conduct seminars in which employees learn how to present and to speak in front of the audience."

T: "So, is it that essentially you'd welcome it if students came equipped with more soft-skills but equally you understand why this is difficult to achieve in academia?"

M2: "Let me say this. The fact is that when graduates start working in our company, they tend to need several months to actually *unlearn* what they have been taught at universities: Namely, to wait for specific orders or exercises, to be passive unless called upon, to stop thinking whether something makes sense or not but rather follow orders, etc., etc. This is absolutely *not* what we need here! So actually we have to re-educate young employees from schools until they overcome the damage done in school education and assimilate the company's culture which is based much on sharing of responsibility and power, and on self-initiative. A few manage this process quite fast and most succeed in a few years, others never arrive and leave us before they have started working. That's what our reality looks like!"

T: "I see. And I can very well imagine what you're saying. This is part of why we're doing this project – hoping to interconnect business, academia and schools and to raise consciousness for what our society needs. Believe me, my teaching as an academic is different. It involves highly interactive concrete projects that, besides assignments, require students' self-initiative and collaboration. Anyway, thank you very much for sharing your perspective, it is essential!"

M2: "Indeed, it would save us a lot of money if students came equipped with other mind-sets and competencies than usual."

Comment
The provocative terms "unlearning" and "re-education" spoke so strongly to us that they got ingrained in our minds and will stay with us for quite some time.

Call: Managers, visit the schools and universities in your neighborhood to give guest-lectures. The students of today will enjoy getting a "practice touch" and may become your employees of tomorrow.

> **Invitation to reflect**
> - Have you ever gone through any unlearning?
> - If so, how did you manage to accomplish it?
> - How can unlearning happen fast, start early, or be prevented at all?

Insights
Education should better avoid emphasizing rigid, fixed constructs and rather focus on problem solving in teams or individually and on critical and appreciative thinking.

Adaptability to new situations is an essential personal capacity, in particular in times of omnipresent change.

Potential strategies
Establish better communication between schools, industry, and academia. Engage actively in knowledge-transfer and establishing contacts via guest lectures, visits, and practice work for students, projects.

Case 4:
Connecting in distributed teams

Keywords: Communication channels, distributed teams, collaboration.

Situation

Real collaboration can be quite challenging in international teams. In the iCom team it was very important to us that the Austrian and Czech part of the team would operate as *one* team, rather than being separate teams with little contact points. Building a team spirit and creating a common vision of what this interdisciplinary, international and boundary-crossing project should be was definitely an essential part of becoming one team. Still, in the everyday work-practice it wasn't always easy to choose the right communication channels that allowed for a valuable exchange about current issues and enabled us to commonly develop ideas while being at distance.

Scenario

The conception and organization of the Practice-Research Workshops was regarded a common task of the whole team. Still, for the workshops organized in or nearby Brno, the Czech part of the team were the lead-organizers, while the Austrian team was mainly responsible for the workshops in Vienna and vicinity. Apart from deciding on dates and locations, the main tasks regarding the workshop conception were choosing a topic, inviting a guest speaker and/or PhD-candidates to present their work, creating a time schedule for the event, choosing or developing a work setting for the small group phases as well as promoting the event. Some of these tasks could easily be organized between the national partners by email interaction and phone calls. Other tasks were more complex. For us it was important that the overall outline and topic for the workshop were decided collaboratively. These tasks were regarded as creative processes and we felt a need for discussing them in the team. Discussions were initiated by uploading documents on Google docs where everyone could include their ideas and give feedback. On the one hand we appreciated the possibility of sharing documents on Google docs and being able to interact through that channel, on the other hand we became aware that it left too much space for uncertainty and misunderstandings. We clearly noticed that the complexity of the discussion (involving many different perspectives and ideas from the team members) required interpersonal, direct communication.

Comment

There could be a saying that "emails are patient" – meaning that in stressful work periods, every email that doesn't involve a clear task or deadline can just too easily remain unanswered. This can cause major frustration in distributed teams, especially when team members rely on each other. We noticed that quite often there was little reaction by team members on group emails that asked for online tasks (such as putting up ideas and providing feedback) without pointing out exactly who is responsible for which task with a clear deadline.

> **Invitation to reflect**
> - If you work in a distributed team, have you had similar experiences with different communication channels?
> - Which channels are the most useful and effective for you?
> - Try to remember a situation where you benefitted from meeting someone in person instead of using technologies – what makes the difference in your perspective?

Insights

When dealing with complex situations or tasks in distributed teams, online-communication can help to gather a lot of different ideas and perspectives.

Creating a common vision or idea in a distributed team through online communication can be a draining process. We noticed that interpersonal, face-to-face communication creates much more energy and dynamic between team members and that we were able to come up with much better concepts and solutions in a shorter period of time. Therefore, although bridging the distance between the two parts of the team was also time consuming, we regarded it as worthwhile to make journeys and get in contact with each other face-to-face. Even just one or a few team members travelling and sharing with others proved helpful.

Potential strategies

Reflect upon the major tasks in your project that require collaboration and critically think about which communication channel would be best suited for each task. You can make a list and agree upon the choice of channel for certain tasks within your team.

Find out whether alternating between face-to-face and online communication can help to get the best out of both means of communication — creative richness balanced with persistent, structured information.

Our insights

"Connecting the dots" enables any form of interaction between people that supports sharing of knowledge and experience and involving different perspectives. We have experienced that practitioners and researchers can provide each other with valuable and useful viewpoints that trigger new ideas. Connecting the dots is about grasping the whole picture or at least getting closer to see it – and this is only possible with the help from others.

Communication technologies enable us to connect with colleagues and business associates over long distances. If a team seeks to get the most benefit from this connection, it has to choose wisely which channels to use for a certain purpose.

Alternating between socially rich face-to-face meetings and more focused virtual channels and spaces has proved that 1+1 can be far more than 2 for connecting the dots while elaborating work products (Motschnig-Pitrik, 2005, 2006; Motschnig-Pitrik and Pitner, 2009; Motschnig-Pitrik and Standl, 2013).

Start soon, young people need and tend to appreciate an authentic look-ahead on the working life. Today's students may become smart co-workers sooner than often imagined.

Next steps to competencies

Do some of these ideas make sense to you?

- Organization
  - Think out of the box! Create a climate of openness where bridging the gap between research and practice is possible.

- Team
  - As a team, think critically about which communication channels are most helpful to you in order to connect with each other and reflect regularly upon the practices you have in place.
  - Seek agreement in the team and offer creative mixtures of communication channels to optimize each person's contribution. Reflect upon the advantages and disadvantages of used communication channels in your team. If in doubt, communicate.

- Personal
  - Be open-minded and approach "outsiders" with different background (from different working contexts, disciplines or even just another department) to receive feedback.
  - Be open to using various communication channels and reflect upon the complications and benefits of the channel of your choice.

Final reflections

In what ways do you agree with these statements?
- If you want to grasp the whole picture, you need different viewpoints.
- Connecting with others is always beneficial.
- The communication channel determines the outcome.
- To aggregate, dots are not enough; you have to connect them.

References

Motschnig-Pitrik, R. (2005). Person-Centered e-Learning in Action: Can Technology help to manifest Person-centered Values in Academic Environments? In: *Journal of Humanistic Psychology, 45* (4), 503-530. SAGE.

Motschnig-Pitrik, R. (2006). Participatory Action Research on a Blended Learning Course on Project Management Soft Skills. In: *Proceedings of 36th Frontiers in Education Conference, (FIE)*. San Diego, CA: IEEE Press.

Motschnig-Pitrik, R., & Pitner, T. (2009). A Person Centered Approach to Including Students in Blended Learning. In: *Proceedings of the 6th SCO (Sharable Content Objects) Conference* (Solka, P., Rambousek, J. (Eds.)). Masaryk University in Brno, June 16-17.

Motschnig-Pitrik, R., & Standl, B. (2013). Person-centered technology enhanced learning: Dimensions of added value. In: *Computers in Human Behavior,* Vol. 29 (2), 401-409.

Knowledge grows from sharing

For a variety of reasons, we often think it is best to keep information to ourselves. Interestingly, when we are courageous enough to share, we may not only find out that others have similar thoughts, but we frequently get back different viewpoints, feelings, ideas concerning the issue at hand – our knowledge grows. More surprisingly, it is not only our own knowledge that extends; knowledge in the whole group can accumulate, expand and grow. Knowledge can also be challenged in a conversation, for example when you need to explain something to others you can find out that there are things that may require further clarification and deeper understanding. In particular, good questions can open up new insights, such as why an employee left your team or what brought your new customer to your website.

Communication can be regarded as a process of constructing and negotiating meaning. It can happen in many different ways in the workplace where colleagues may:
- Update each other on the progress/stumbling stones of their projects;

- Thoroughly explain certain problems;
- Analyze reasons for arising difficulties;
- Share good practice;
- Ask critical questions about decisions that have been made or they may get together to share ideas and inspirations.

All of these communicative practices help to create new insights and meanings and can contribute substantially to a successful project implementation. A person who deliberately keeps information from others can be regarded as a major obstacle for advancement and innovation. Establishing an attentive listening practice and an open climate that promotes knowledge sharing are therefore key success factors for any organization.

So, what is it that contributes to a climate that motivates people to share with others? And, if employees are willing to share, what steps (in terms of structures, events, places, opportunities, etc.) need to be taken so that sharing actually does happen and teams or organizations can benefit from it?

Keywords: Atmosphere, work climate, generating knowledge, learning together, learning from cases, flat hierarchy, process approach, collaboration.

Cases

Overview of cases

- Case 1 **"Doing away with hierarchy and walls"** provides a glimpse at how knowledge can grow in a pleasant atmosphere off-site where managers and scientists share their experience by exchanging opinions and strategies on how to make communication more constructive.

- Case 2 **"Processes as enablers of efficient knowledge transfer"** investigates the ways in which specific processes are "enablers of effective knowledge transfer."

- Case 3 **"How can we find the most appropriate person?"** takes up the decisive situation of a job interview and illustrates how practitioners and scientists collaborate to make humanistic theory directly applicable to practice.

The final part of the topic opens up a repertoire of settings for knowledge sharing aiming at guiding managers in their choice of a particular setting.

Case 1:
Doing away with hierarchy and walls

Keywords: Atmosphere, work climate, generating knowledge, learning together, learning from cases, flat hierarchy.

Situation
In the Practice-Research Workshops we organized, we took an effort to establish an open and respectful atmosphere so that the participants feel comfortable and safe. It was then possible to get deeper insights into the personal experience of the business partners. Active listening and authenticity helped to establish such an environment. At the workshop carried out in Chvalovice we, in particular, experienced the influence the location has on a "sharing atmosphere". The conversations there were very open, deep, positive and at eye level. Surprisingly, the participants opened up very quickly and shared their business practices, negative experiences and stories of success. This positive atmosphere was often manifested in conversations in small groups but also during the breaks.

Scenario
The above-mentioned workshop in Chvalovice, a small town in the Czech Republic near the Austrian border, was carried out in a pleasant location in the countryside surrounded by vineyards. During the two days of conversations, presentations, dialogues and personal exchange we identified a common ground of practice, research and education and how they can work together and benefit from each other. This trust-inspiring environment was perceived by a business participant as follows:

Participant 1: "The atmosphere was very pleasant throughout the whole workshop. I felt really welcomed."

This underlines that the welcoming climate was identified as an important factor of feeling comfortable. Another precondition of an environment where everyone feels safe was identified as the democratic structure of the workshops:

Participant 2: "There were no levels – it did not matter if you were a leader, professor, PhD, or whatever." This shows that the flat organization and structure of the workshop was important for the participants to open up and feel involved.

Another participant specified in his feedback why it was possible to open up and share business experience with other business partners, researchers and participants.

Participant 3: "People should be open – you shouldn't be hiding anything, you should be willing to share. Still, the setting helped a lot. If you feel that others might misuse the information, then you eventually stop sharing or start pretending that your company is just perfect. But when the circumstances are favorable to sharing, it really helps to talk about problems – this helps to summarize, structure and define the problem and to elaborate on what could help to solve it."

This climate allowed the participants to identify new insights.

Participant 4: "Now I see more clearly that allowing employees to access project information directly would make communication channels simpler and more reliable."
Other participants liked his ideas and shared what they perceived as too time consuming in *their* organizations' reporting procedures.

During a break another participant remarked that he would like to come to another workshop but had no time. He realized that it would be great for his company if at least one of its representatives could attend the workshop. He suggested his manager should come – and she did (see case 3 in this topic). But not only managers got new insights from this workshop. A colleague from the iCom team said: "Now I see the goals of my thesis much clearer – my research can reveal more about the management of ICT-projects if I start at the top – with the companies' management – rather than researching the team. During one of the breaks a manager hit the nail on the head when he said the fish smells from its head." Indeed, this proved to be a valuable insight. Experiences such as those described above point to the fact that the combination of a positive climate, clear communication structures, and no hierarchy positively influence the growth of knowledge through sharing.

Comment
The organization of the practice research workshops changed during the three years when they took place. Sometimes we tried a more formal environment, and sometimes a friendlier one.

Invitation to reflect
- Have you ever been worried that you have told a person too much about your business?
- How could you organize an informal meeting where you can share experience without having to worry about being disadvantaged by doing so?

Insights
The workshops revealed that participants open up and feel comfortable if the event has a flat structure, takes place in a nice surrounding outside the usual business environment and is well facilitated.

Case 2:
Processes as enablers of efficient knowledge transfer

Keywords: Process approach, collaboration, transparency, integrating new hires.

Situation
This case was recorded during a process analysis project done at a Small and Medium Enterprise (SME) sized Software Company (let's call it SWC). The company grew very quickly from a start-up to SME size and a more formal codification of its internal processes was needed. We identified one significant problem during the initial interviews with the company management. The "QA & Application Maintenance" department had a very poor knowledge of the work processes in the Development Department and vice versa.

Scenario
Such a "knowledge gap" was considered the source of problems and inefficiencies during the implementation and testing of the new features requested by the company's key customer. After a discussion with the management, we came to the conclusion that the roots of this problem reached several years back, when the company was small and all the testing and Quality Assurance (QA) was done by the development. Internal employees of the key customer did the maintenance. Later, these internal employees were transferred from customer to SWC and formed the "QA and Application Maintenance" department, but then several newcomers staffed the area. The new people obviously did not know a lot about the development process of the software product. The second phase of the process analysis involved process mapping and consequent modeling in the Business Process Model and Notation (BPMN). To fill the identified "knowledge gap", we decided to organize process mapping interviews in 4 half-day workshops. During each workshop we invited employees from one of the departments to be interviewed and several people from the other department to act as "observers". According to the information gathered during those workshops we modeled all the processes from both departments, assembled them together into an "end-to-end process" and described the relationships among its sub-processes. The resulting documents were sent to both departments to get some feedback so they could be discussed in detail at the final 1-day workshop. During this workshop, both departments

explained their work processes to each other in detail. Additionally, there were several suggestions from both sides on how to improve the collaboration to save effort on both sides.

Comment
The final discussion led to a complete clarification of all the processes on both sides, which then resulted in a sustainable and mutual understanding of the processes and consequently in an improvement of collaboration among the departments.

> **Invitation to reflect**
> - Activities described in this case require the process participants to give them some extra time.
> - Can you see any long-term benefits of such clarification or do you consider it a waste of employees' time?
> Does it make sense to let others know what are my duties if I am the only one responsible for my part of the process?
> - How does it improve collaboration? How can we codify such know-how to make it understandable to others?

Insights
Obviously, at least a basic knowledge of the "end-to-end process" can be beneficial. I can collaborate with others much better if I know "how they work". I can substitute other people as well as delegate some of my work to others if we share some common knowledge of the "parent process".

Potential strategies
Try to make at least the "big picture" of the work process public. When people know the process well, they can share ideas and experience and work together to improve it. Document your processes to codify the know-how, thus allowing people to talk about them and learn them faster. Be open to suggestions concerning improvement of the process, even if they come from people who are not directly involved in the particular process. Different points of view can often prove to be beneficial.

Case 3:
How can we find the most appropriate person?

Job interviews and a person-centered attitude

Keywords: Job interview, person-centered qualities, communication, listening, empathy.

Situation
During a Practice-Research Workshop, some researchers and ICT-managers met in a small dialogue group to find out how person-centered theory could help to address major challenges arising from practice. One such challenge is the responsibility of a manager to carry out job interviews with prospective team members. As the fate of a successful team lies with each and every of its members, the selection of new team members is a sensitive process with a great impact. While it seems easy to assess the candidates' factual knowledge it appears to be a lot harder to accurately perceive his/her interpersonal qualities. However, for a positive, beneficial team climate such qualities are known to be even more important than factual knowledge, which can be obtained relatively easily. This case shows how knowledge of interpersonal concepts can be connected to situations, which can play a decisive role in practice.

Scenario
At the beginning of the group conversation it turned out that it would be basically possible to consider person-centered theories for job interviews. Based on the three attitudes of realness, respect, and deep understanding, the small group considered how a job interview could be designed to be as authentic and respectful as possible. One participant (the supervisor of the employee having attended the workshop in Chvalovice – see Case 1 in this topic) mentioned that a job interview in such a positive climate was certainly beneficial for both parties. She said: "It's simply a fact that a conversation without facade, where everybody communicates openly and transparently, is more satisfying for both partners because you know exactly how a future collaboration can work or not." She referred to the humanistic attitudes that can establish a climate where a holistic experience of the other person is possible. A further step towards an authentic job interview would be to include the entire team in the meeting with the candidate. This

participant wondered: "Why do we still need tests and an assessment center, if empathy and authenticity can already reveal so much?" The multitude of perceptions of how the interview went and whether the candidate would fit into the team could reveal much more about him/her than just the manager's impression.

Comment

This case outlines a typical setting of the Practice-Research Workshops as we carried them out. It is an example of how participants from both practice and research can benefit from each other, connect and share their views, given a constructive climate and an appropriate setting is provided. However, this requires time and will and can succeed only if people are willing to invest it.

> **Invitation to reflect**
> - Try to recall one or two job interviews you attended as an interviewer or as an applicant. How would have a high degree of honesty, respect, pursuit of deeper understanding of the other party and the circumstances changed the interviews?
> - Plan your next job interview along these qualities. What would your interview guideline look like if you tried to deeply understand the applicant or employee and talk with him/her openly and with respect?

Insights

Sometimes, theory seems to be far away from practice. Job interviews can be difficult for both sides. If you make yourself aware of the underlying psychological concepts you can improve your understanding of what is going on during the interview.

A really useful theory needs to be applicable in real life/job situations! Theoreticians alone cannot establish applications. The connection to practice requires dialogue between researchers and practitioners. Typically, both parties can learn from each other while being part of such a dialogue.

Our insights

We have found out that sharing knowledge and experience is an integral part of every well-functioning team. Whether the shared knowledge is factual or concerns skills and personality, it is important to share knowledge within a beneficial climate and in an appropriate way. But sharing knowledge is not a one-way process. It is an interdependent system of providing and perceiving; an environment where *each* participant can feel comfortable to give and receive information, thus growing both as a person and as a professional.

In the iCom project we experienced various settings of sharing and found out that each is particularly fitting for a certain purpose but less so for others. Hence, the following table is intended to provide an overview of various settings for sharing and assist the reader with choosing the most appropriate one given their particular task at hand.

Setting/ features	Structure	Process	Topic	Major envisaged outcome
Interactive presentation	Highly structured	Rather linear and defined	Predefined by organizer	Increase in information regarding a thematic field or topic
Panel discussion	From structured to unstructured at the end	Predefined	Predefined by organizer	Experts' views on some issue
World-Café	Highly structured	Inter-woven and defined	Predefined by organizer	Coming up with new ideas and broadening horizons
Open case	Loosely structured	Moderated and defined	Thematic scope communicated in advance	Sharing experience on some particular problem, insight, solution strategies
Open space	Very loosely structured	Moderated with defined structure & free slots	Thematic scope determined by participants ad hoc	Sharing ideas and interests; any goal identified by the session moderator
Small team dialogue	Typically unstructured	Typically open	Loosely defined	Detailed elaboration, extended knowledge and intensified relationships
Encounter group	Unstructured	Facilitated and undefined	Meeting person-to-person, theme may be communicated in advance	Personal growth, group experience, community building

Table 2: Overview of settings for creating knowledge and experience

Next steps to competencies

Do some of the following ideas make sense to you?

- Organization
  - Organize a meeting of people with similar business experience and try to establish a beneficial workshop climate. Why not meet in a vineyard?

- Team
  - Share your experience, visions and problems with a colleague you feel already comfortable with. Meet as a team on a regular basis as well as on occasion.

- Individual
  - Start with small steps. Sometimes it is not easy to open up and share knowledge in a larger group from the very beginning. Is there anything you wish others would know about you or your work? If so, look for an occasion to share.
  - Listen attentively to others and make an effort to make sense of their message. Tell them in your own words what is the gist of what you heard.

Final reflections

In what ways do you agree with these statements?
- The degree of feeling comfortable in a group decides on how open you will be.
- Sharing knowledge with colleagues increases the team knowledge.
- Sometimes less is more – but nothing is definitely too little.
- Listening is at least as important as voicing your opinion.
- A true dialogue unfolds best in an atmosphere of openness and trust.

References

Bohm, G. (1996). *On dialogue.* New York: Routledge.
Motschnig, R., & Nykl, L. (2014). *Person-centred Communication: Theory, Skills & Practice.* Open University Press.
Nykl, L., & Motschnig-Pitrik, R. (2002). *Uniting Rogers' and Vygotsky's Theories on Personality and Learning.* On: *Carl Rogers Conference 2002.* San Diego, USA.

Learning Organization

Every perspective is valuable

Whether confirming or disproving, every (honest) perspective can get you closer to the "truth", if only you consider it. **Different viewpoints help us to gain a differentiated view of a certain situation and can enable us to see the "big picture".**

In particular, complex situations or decisions tend to benefit from a multi-perspective rather than single-perspective view. As is common truth: 4 eyes see more than 2 eyes, and, in particular, persons of different background, position, gender, age, etc. tend to contribute to a more holistic, real, and hence accurate impression of any complex phenomenon.

In organizations, the management board can benefit from considering the perspectives of other employees and involving them at early stages of complex decision-making or change processes. Involving does not only mean informing people about a decision to be made or already made, but to collect their opinions and insights on the topic. Often, people who work with a system, a process, or a stakeholder every day know better where things can be improved.

Making decisions which ignore the needs of employees often leads to solutions which don't correspond with the work routines of employees (or even customers) and as a result are not accepted or followed. **Whenever there is complexity, leading requires recognizing that other perspectives (across hierarchies) might help to find the best solutions.**

For more information about dealing with employees' ideas, see chapters *"Meeting at eye level opens doors"* and *"Communication matters, cultivate it"*.

Keywords: Person-Product-Profit, listening, learning together, dialogue, meeting at eye level, inclusion, unconditional positive regard, empathy, getting closer, decision-making.

Cases

Overview of cases

- Case 1 **"Group-discussion about excursion (The "Donauinsel" situation)"** deals with the decision-making process in groups – when it is valuable to take into account opinions of all participants to reach a compromise or when it is better to let the majority decide.

- Case 2 **"Include those who are really affected"** describes the situation when employees were neither informed nor involved into the strategic decision to move the organization into another building which caused their frustration.

- Case 3 **"Putting together the iCom project proposal"** shows how you can learn a lot from failures – it describes the "two-step" process of submitting the iCom project proposal. After the rejection, the iCom team concentrated all efforts and started to work not as a single person but as a collective, which led to final acceptance.

Case 1:
Group-discussion about excursion (The "Donauinsel" situation)

Keywords: Decision-making process in groups, compromise.

Situation
During the 1st PhD-course on "International Constructive Communication" the afternoon of the 3rd day was reserved for an outdoor activity such that participants could get to know each other also outside of the seminar room. The sun was shining; our conversations in the course had taken already longer than expected such that the lunch break was overdue.

Scenario
The facilitator suggested to stop the discussion at that point and asked the group where they wanted to spend the afternoon, including the lunch break. It was suggested by the facilitator to make an excursion to the Danube Island – a public recreation area that offers lots to do.

Among the course participants, there were different preferences on how to spend the afternoon and where to have lunch. Some of us just wanted to grab a quick at a supermarket, others wanted to have a bigger lunch. Some wanted to go there riding rental bikes but weren't sure about where they could rent them, others preferred public transport. Then it wasn't clear where exactly the group would meet up, as the Danube Island is a big area.

More and more participants suggested their ideal way of getting there – during the process some created specific expectations whereas others started to get bored and annoyed (also influenced by a feeling of hunger). As nobody decided finally, but every perspective was discussed and involved, it took about 30 minutes to decide how to proceed.

Course participant A: "I actually had no time for the lunch break as I had to finish a proposal that was due on that day. Therefore, it would have been stressful for me to go to the Danube Island (it takes around half an hour to get there) and I preferred to stay in the office to finish my proposal. I perceived the long discussion about how to spend the lunch break and the afternoon as well as what medium of transport to use as a time-consuming process. To me, it was not an effective way to make a decision about a rather unimportant issue. I felt that the discussion was "wasting" my (and others' time)."

Course participant B: "I generally see the benefits of involving a whole team in the decision-making process; I still think this mainly applies to major decisions during projects or processes. Trying to involve all team members at all times might cause resignation. The decision we had to make in this case was minor and I think that it was rather unimportant for the majority of the team members. Instead of forcing the creation of a consensus, the facilitator should have made the decision for the group based on the preferences of the majority. Actually such long decision-making processes can get really painful as they both consume time and energy that could be invested in more important things. Also in my view, people expect the leader to provide at least a framework or fragmental structure."

Comment

The facilitator tried to consider every preference and find responses for every question while in the meantime some participants got bored and hungry and started to express their frustration with the lengthy process. There was no convergence of suggestions for quite some time such that participants simply left to have lunch. They knew when they were expected to be back and somehow trusted that they might find the others at the Danube Island. Nobody seemed satisfied with the outcome, and negative feelings about the lack of organization prevailed.

Invitation to reflect
- In your view, what was the major problem?
- Did you ever experience a similar situation?
- If you were the facilitator, how would you react?
- How would you react if you were a participant in such a situation?
- What do you think that the group members and the facilitator might have learned from the situation?
- How can you make a good decision in reasonable time?

Insights

Not every decision requires the consensus of all persons involved, sometimes it's good to just let the majority decide from choices presented by the leader. Reaching consensus or negotiating a compromise may cost too much time and not be the preferred path.

The time and effort must be in balance with potential benefits that the long discussion process can bring for the "common good".

Ideas for handling the case
- Keep it simple. Allow time for exchange of different perspectives, consider varying opinions and preferences in the decision-making process.
- It can be a good idea to define a time frame for bringing up ideas. After that first phase make use of an effective decision-making process.
- The group could vote and then follow the decision of the majority. It could alternatively assign the right to make the decision to one or more persons during the first phase of the decision-making process.
- The assigned leaders can then act in what they believe is in the best interest for the group.

Case 2:
Include those who are really affected

Keywords: End-user inclusion, participation, job-satisfaction, hierarchy.

Situation
New office space was acquired and furnished. As one of the departments moved to the new place, most of the moved employees weren't really happy. Is it fair to ask: Should they be?

Scenario
Just a few weeks before relocating, the employees received the information concerning exactly where their new office space would be. The offices were equipped depending on the position and the employment-status of persons within the department. Organizational hierarchies were the primary criterion on office space and equipment allocation; requests for changes were not accepted in the initial placement. Strict rules were set up as to the placement and operation of any further devices and equipment.

Moving to the new place went smoothly. Employees enjoyed certain facets of the new offices but many complained about the hierarchic and anti-social procedures, commenting about the waste of resources due to standard equipment and in some cases inappropriate allocation. They just were not really happy at all and, consequently, not energized to work in the new environment. They felt it been set upon them like a "golden cage" with several faults and no previous communication about several aspects of such a change.

Comment

On the one hand, the strategy to minimize complexity and confusion worked really well; on the other hand, as employees' ideas and requirements were ignored, morale was hurt. The net outcome of this strategy for the department will need to be assessed later and/or by each observer and "player" individually.

Invitation to reflect

- Do you contemplate the agenda, hidden or not, as to why the management decided to equip the rooms "a standardized way" like in this case?
- Have you experienced a situation in which you were asked for your view or contribution, however, at a very late stage? How did you feel and react?
- Are there any general dynamics that you discovered when reading the case?
- What is your view and experience on including end-users in decisions affecting their work environment?

Insights

Things are easier to criticize if you were not part of the design team and were not asked.

Things are harder to accept if they come from an external frame of thought, and there was no way to be involved in the decision or execution process.

Standardized solutions can be accepted if there is a clarification of the purpose of some (design) decision behind them.

Potential strategies

- Include those who are affected early if acceptance matters.
- At least inform them and share the constraints of the project if you want to prevent confrontation later.

Case 3:
Putting together the iCom project proposal

Keywords: Listening, external viewpoint, regional strategies, common sense, sensing.

Situation
The initial iCom project proposal was put together between researchers and academic staff of two universities. After the first application for funding, the proposal was rejected and the team was asked to revise the proposal and hand it in again.

Scenario
Preparing a successful project is often not a straightforward process. Very few proposals are accepted on the first try. There is usually a kind of learning from experience, taking the evaluator's reviews but also personal experience from the preparation process which lead to improved proposal. However, in the case of iCom, the evolution of the proposal was twofold, as the project proposal preparation included a lot of explanatory work also towards the evaluators. The idea of such an "academic" interdisciplinary project was almost completely new for the agencies involved in proposal evaluation and selection process.

Shortly after notification, the iCom team was a bit disappointed but equally energized: We can resubmit, the reviewers' comments make sense, we need to better consider the regional strategies. This is what we're going to do, and we will make it!

A meeting was arranged with the technical secretariat. Three persons from the Austrian team attended the meeting, and the referee told us openly where the decision-making body had problems, what they just didn't understand, and what needed to be improved. We listened carefully, made notes, shared our ideas on possible remedies and immediately started on putting together the next version. Something similar happened on the Czech team's side, and we met to exchange information. The technical secretariat invited us to workshops for proposers and workshops for sharing among project holders.

Later, shortly before the submission date, we kindly asked a person from the technical secretariat to let us know whether the proposal was written in an understandable style. On the next day we were surprised to hear how many issues and abbreviations just weren't clear. But we were clear about the fact that this was precious information, and we spent the night working on a rephrasing for understandability by non-experts in our field.

Listening to our minds and hearts and to the views and suggestions by others was our key to success. The proposal was accepted. Not a single person but a collective, thoughtful mind was needed – and we are grateful for this experience.

Comment
The combined energy was a major vehicle in the success. Looking back, the team was grateful that the first proposal was not accepted since the whole effort could have been a lot more complex. The team quickly began their socialization to the iterative communication processes necessary to conceptualize, communicate, and execute such a complex project.

> **Invitation to reflect**
> - Is there any "rule of thumb" or heuristic how much listening is helpful with policy makers?
> - Can you and your team(s) be grateful for the effects of unwelcome news?
> - Is there a point when too much listening and adapting draws one away from one's own ideas and motivations?

Insights
Simply, every perspective is valuable. Whether one or two is most valuable will differ from case to case and needs some kind of "empathy to the whole situation", which requires careful sensing and reflection. The whole process needs time to allow proposals (and other "things") to form, but may require quick action at other points to fit external parameters.

Potential strategies
Get in contact. Seek feedback actively, even if, or especially if, the feedback may be negative but the stakeholder is crucial to the success of the project.

When participating in formal application processes, such as preparing a proposal for public funding or competing in a tender for innovative ideas, don't hesitate to approach persons who might be able to provide you with valuable knowledge. Nowadays, many projects are highly specific and interdisciplinary. Anyone can have blind spots and regard knowledge as common sense that is described in terms not understandable by the general public. Get an outsider's opinion on it.

- How do you perceive these situations? Did you ever face a similar situation? How did you solve it?
- Honestly, how do you feel when your suggestion is rejected by the organization/team? How do you feel when you are not asked about a situation that has a major impact on your work life? Or when you and teamates cannot decide on a decision that has little impact on your work life?
- Are you annoyed? Do you conclude that your suggestions or the approach to decision-making was not perfect and take it as a learning experience and opportunity to improve?

Our insights

Every perspective is valuable and it is important to consider the multitude of opinions and ideas in work processes. This might be trying to find creative solutions, putting together a proposal for an innovative project, or making decisions about where to spend a team meeting. Still, we have to accept that not every decision will always meet everyone's expectations. The cases above show that involving the whole team yet finding common sense during a decision-making process is important in decisions that have significant consequences for people.

Next steps to competencies

Do the following ideas make sense to you?

- Organization
  - Don't make strategic decisions without people which are the most influenced by them. When coming back to Case 2, it is a common practice that all employees are informed about pros and cons of moving to another building and then all of them can vote or at least speak their mind. This process not always leads to the option preferred by the management but what is better – to have a beautiful new building or satisfied employees? Also, sometimes employees will vote for the new building but then can give simple feedback on what they do not like about it when it is easier to fix or are innoculated against the parts they do not like so that they are better prepared to accept them if the feedback cannot be utilized by the management.

- Team
  - Distinguish between important and less important issues which should be discussed in the team. Generally people love to be involved in the decision process – it makes them feel important. But they also have to feel that the issue is important enough and that they will have some impact. Otherwise it can have an opposite effect – long discussions about less important decisions start to be tedious and people can even have an impression that the manager is unable or incompetent to decide anything on his or her own.

- Individual
  - Try to be a part of the decision process when you feel that your opinion can be really valuable. Don't complicate the situation with unreasonable complaints and try to help your superiors to come to a satisfiable decision. Be patient, it is always complicated to satisfy all people involved.

Final reflections

In what ways do you agree with these statements?
- The team leader has to make the final decision.
- Asking for different perspectives doesn't necessarily mean that all of them will be equally considered.
- Only by considering all perspectives one can guarantee ideal strategic decisions in teams.

The team is the most wonderful place to learn

What do we mean by **team**? Here it is the people around you with whom you share a couple of goals and interests. Typically you work on some project(s) together but this is not necessarily so.

In the context of teams or peer groups, the term **"to learn"** is used in a very broad sense **including any process leading to some enhancement or change of knowledge, skills, behavior, values, or relationships.**

As complexity in the world is increasing and knowledge is created and re-created at high speed, it has become impossible for a single human being to "know it all". **In order to be successful in business and life, it seems inevitable to connect with others, to involve the knowledge of work colleagues as well as external partners** (see also topics: *"Connect the dots"* and *"Knowledge grows from sharing"*).

The team is a unique social system that brings different people together to engage in a common challenge. In this focused environment, people get in contact with different viewpoints, habits, and personality traits and can learn from one another's ways of dealing with problems, approaching and engaging in situations and a lot more. **People can learn intellectually on their job, and further in their interpersonal skills.** In the following cases, several facets of team situations are presented that demonstrate key learnings of team participants in various areas that were only possible through the special environment a team offers.

In the following you'll find some responses to questions like:
- What kind of (unique) learning happens in a good team or group?
- How can one cultivate a team or group to be a wonderful place to be part of and to learn?

Keywords: Dealing with conflict, team decision-making, dialogue, role-play, empathic listening, meetings.

Cases

Overview of cases

- Case 1 **"Making it right for everybody"** explores the difficulties of team decision-making in a workshop setting, even when experienced facilitators are present. Moderating a discussion can be challenging.

- Case 2 **"What a demanding character!?"** illustrates how teams can provide learning opportunities to broaden moderating skills, in both real-life or role-play.

- Case 3 **"Do YOU have a support group?"** describes how just a short dialogue can inspire team spirit.

- Case 4 **"When informal works well…"** reveals that trying to formalize and broaden the number of participants of informal meetings can block productivity and spontaneous learning experiences.

- Case 5 **"Schools can help develop team skills"** emphasizes the necessity of starting to develop team skills at schools.

- Case 6 **"Loneliness on the top"** gives a short reflection of a situation that is very common in top management – the feeling that there is no one to share experience and problems with.

Case 1:
Making it right for everybody

"Each one of us was responsible for the workshop, thus supported to become a kind of a leader. That is great on one hand, but can perhaps result in more frustration if it doesn't go as well as one wished."

A participant in the 4th PhD-course

Keywords: Conflict, communication, decision-making, shared vision, dialogue, workshop, schedule, empathic understanding, informal meeting.

Scenario

From November, 21st – 23rd, 2012 the 4th iCom PhD-course was held in cooperation with the Faculty of Informatics (Masaryk University) in Brno. The course offer was designed for doctorate candidates in the field of Informatics and Business Informatics, but also available to business partners from the iCom project in order to include a practical perspective.

The course was facilitated by visiting lecturer Antonio Monteiro dos Santos (Brazil/USA), Professor Renate Motschnig (University of Vienna), Priv.-Doz. Nino Tomaschek (Postgraduate Center/University of Vienna) and Professor Tomáš Pitner (Masaryk University Brno).

Besides content-related inputs on "learning organizations", "innovation", and "wise intelligence" in the context of new communication media, the course allowed the international participants to elaborate the principles of a learning organization based on practical cases in small work groups and to reflect critically on the characteristics and demands of such an organization.

In the course, people from heterogeneous contexts, from academia and industry, with different expectations, participated for an individually varying amount of time. The facilitators offered multiple perspectives on the complex concept "learning organization" reaching from systems-theory viewpoints to organizational psychology and self-experience as a basis for generative learning. Facilitators wanted to provide a significant course experience and, thus, included the course group extensively in decisions on course contents to be elaborated and the time schedule of course blocks. In the reflection sheets after the course, many participants shared that they perceived long discussions over the course schedule to be exhausting and not contributing to an ideal work atmosphere. They introduced a broad range of activities, theory, and opportunities for self-experience in the context of learning organizations which was experienced as intense or demanding.

Comment

> **Edith:**
> "These experiences of learning as a team, creating visions, setting goals, working towards the goals and handling problems, might be conflicting at times as team members have contrary opinions on specific issues or set their priorities differently. The process of negotiating meaning and priorities is important and entails a lot of creative potential, e.g. finding new concepts for workshops or new ideas for collaborative work. … I feel we need faster decision-making processes and also in workshops, I think that clear time frames and guidelines are necessary. Within these structures we can then allow for extensive openness and freedom. The experiences of previous workshops and the PhD-course show me that it is hard to keep a highly diverse group of students, entrepreneurs, and employees from the private or public sector interested as well as active without providing them with a clear structure and an outlook on learning outcomes. I feel that even the idea of self-organized teams can be beneficial in workshops if there is still someone who steers the learning and working processes, someone who provides orientation. Otherwise a lot of time might be used or even "wasted" discussing basic organizational questions, withdrawing energy from the group that could well be used more productively."

> **Renate:**
> "Some impressions that stayed with me:
> - It does not suffice to bring together experienced facilitators who each have a lot of exciting 'issues' to share. They need to form a shared vision what & how course goals are to be achieved.
> - An unsteady group of participants who all bring quite high expectations is a particular challenge. The group can't form if it changes constantly and thus group norms can't unfold. This, for example, affects decision-making processes in a ways that convergence is much harder to be achieved than in a group that has established some kind of patterns of likes and dislikes.
> - Preparing and providing material on the learning platform doesn't suffice – reading and elaborating needs to be inspired in some way.
> - Trying to build a shared vision when participants are overloaded with work and, furthermore, prefer new theory inputs, doesn't have a fair chance to succeed.
> - Self-experience seems to be valued less high than a lecture by a significant number of colleagues, in particular, if time is quite short."

Antonio:
"I am always fascinated by how people can work together and in such a small chunk of time learn, set up goals, create their own visions, handle all different kinds of problems that emerge in a certain situation as in the situation presented by our course. It is important to know that every group that forms goes through phases such as the phase of meeting and getting to know each other, learning how to handle one another, beginning to trust and learning how to work as a group. There is also what I call the infernal phase where conflicts emerge and we are tested to our limits to find creative ways of resolving conflicts in a caring way. And finally begins the process of departing and separating from people with whom we bonded for some hours or even some days, more with some than others, and that perhaps we are never going to see again. This happens whether this is the first time that we are meeting or even if we have met before. A sensitivity of the professor to those aspects of any class can enrich the class and can open the student to learn new ways to cope with his environment. I believe this happened in our course.

From my experience of more than 20 years working in different settings including school and organizational settings is that the more technically oriented we are, the more uncomfortable we are with being non-directive. However being non-directive can open professors and students for a different dimension of human experience and provide managers and employees with the skill to deal with the most unexpected situations that always appear in their lives and work environment within schools and organizations.

This does not mean that the directive way is less important because the directive way can help us save time and be more direct with certain aspects of the learning environment as we have concluded from our courses. However, it has been overused and when that happens it blocks creativity, wisdom and compassion tremendously. In my experience as a professor and consultant in organizations, in such courses as the one we taught, it is important to reach a balance between working in a structured and unstructured way. I believe our class was an example of that."

Jan:
"When it comes to the process of our workshop, I'm quite content. I appreciate to see how people firstly share their expectations, discuss, think, and only after that listen to some theory and cases."

Christina:
"I think it is not goal-oriented at all to have the group discuss how long we should do a break or similar small decisions. I don't feel that it would be very directive to suggest one or two options and let the group pick one (democratically) and/or adapt the options if the group is not satisfied with neither. I think it makes sense to have big decisions, the general orientation of a project and visions, strategies and goals, as well as big changes, discussed in the team – even if it takes long to decide. But if everybody feels involved in the decision-making process for big decisions, I think, it can be very beneficial for daily work, but also for a company's project. On the other hand, minor decisions should be done, in my opinion, by the leader/manager or democratically (majority decides) for some reasons. These would be my hypotheses and observations:
- *Open facilitation is not always likely to generate consensus on every topic. Also, participative management does not necessarily mean consensus ...*
- *Such minor decisions are unlikely to jeopardize the success of a project/company.*
- *I personally perceive these minor group decisions as very energy consuming and stressful and I would expect the manager to take responsibility for such minor decisions."*

Invitation to reflect
- Would a strict schedule have brought about better learning experiences for participants?
- Is including all participants in basic decisions in a group worthwhile?
- What does it look like in a project team context?
- What is the most productive decision-making strategy in a team for you?

Insights

Although the opportunity to contribute to the course structure supported a sense of self-responsibility in group members, leadership directives were wished for in times of extensive disagreement.

Facilitators profit from clarifying personal visions and goals in the setting with each other before working with the group.

Long periods of undecidedness without direction, contradiction, or disagreement, were experienced as fatiguing and frustrating, but yielded considerations on how to design an optimal teamwork setting.

Complex issues can be tackled well in a peer group or team. All participants in the course of our case could speak of personally significant learning experiences. Though, the myth of making it right for everybody is doomed to break, when group members are enabled to voice their thoughts and feelings on complex situations.

Case 2:
What a demanding character!?

A team can be the most wonderful place to learn, but it is not always easy. According to the feedback of iCom participants, guided case-based learning settings in small groups have proven to be highly beneficial. However, sometimes guiding such groups can be challenging for the moderator of the group.

Keywords: Moderation, workshop, role-play, facilitation, reflection, empathic understanding.

Situation
In one of the iCom workshops we experienced that a single participant in a group setting may drain attention from the learning process of the whole group. While the participants of the group started to share experiences from their work context and collaboratively tried to develop a deeper understanding of one specific situation, one participant demanded extensive attention for a different topic of personal interest. For the moderator of the group it was challenging to attend to the needs of this one person while also regarding the needs of all other participants who seemed to have more interest in developing further understanding of a particular work situation that was shared. Also the participant demanded answers and solutions to specific questions from the moderator, which was not part of the parameters for the group work.

A few days after the workshop the group settings of the workshop were reflected in an iCom team meeting, and the moderator of this group shared the challenging experience.

Scenario

The iCom team member was interested in developing her moderation skills when a demanding person is part of the group to moderate, but the workshop was already over. After the team member shared her frustration, the team offered to play through the situation in a role-play so she could re-examine her feelings and interactions. The moderator took on the role of the participant and another team member played the moderator.

The following dialogue is based on experiences of iCom team members that reflected on the role-play and demonstrates how such a role-play could be done:

Anne, Max, Rose & Sophie (iCom team members)
Workshop-group members are discussing a work situation, trying to understand the context of it.

Anne to *Max*: "I would really like to know how I can apply 'Theory A' – which was presented in the plenary – in my work context."

Max to *Anne*: "Well, I can provide you with literature on 'Theory A', so you can study more on it. As I am not an expert on 'Theory A', I cannot provide you with an answer but maybe someone from the group has ideas on this."

Anne to *Max*: "Ok, but you mentioned in that speech before that 'Theory A' consists of five factors... can you say more about this?"

Max to *Anne*: "If you like, we can talk about this in the break. The group session is supposed to provide space for sharing work experiences related to the topic of 'ABC' and I suggest we continue with the work situation that participant C started to describe before."

Anne to *Max*: "Ok, but I thought this workshop was on 'Theory A', and I would really like to know more about it."

Max to *Anne*: "I can give you a list of follow-up literature and send you some notes on the topic, but we cannot talk about it right now."

Anne to *Max* (annoyed and disappointed): "Ok."

After the role-play, iCom team members shared impressions, thoughts and feelings concerning this situation in the context of the workshop setting.

Rose to *Anne*: "How was this situation for you as the participant now? How did you feel?"

Anne to the team: "I was really interested in 'Theory A'. When the moderator constantly told me that we can't talk about it now, I felt really rejected."

Rose to *Max*: "How was it for you in the role of the moderator?"

Max to the team: "Really annoying. I could not focus on what the team wanted to elaborate. Nor did I find time to deal appropriately with the participant."

Anne to *Max*: "I felt as if you would not take me seriously, as if you would misunderstand me or not hear me out in my needs. Maybe this is why the participant insisted to talk about 'Theory A'?"

Sophie to *Anne* and *Max*: "You appeared to be angry."

Anne to *Sophie*: "Yes, I really felt angry and upset."

Max to *Anne*: "I had a responsibility to the whole group and the designated task, but maybe I could have listened more carefully to what you said and were trying to communicate about your needs and interest. Would that have made a difference?"

Anne to *Max*: "I think so. Maybe as a moderator in the group, I could have asked the other participants whether they want to follow up on the topic proposed by this participant. This broader feedback to the participant maybe would have released some pressure."

Comment

Engaging in this short role-play proved to be highly effective in understanding the feelings, actions and expectations of this participant. Also, it helped to understand what the moderator's responses might have caused in this certain participant.

The reflection of the role-play within the iCom team was a valuable learning experience for everyone in the iCom team. Sharing this specific challenge in the team and getting colleagues involved in the case made it possible for the moderator to collaboratively develop possible solution strategies together. This sort of learning process would not have been possible alone.

For the group moderator, one possibility to deal with the situation would have been to attend to the participant involving the whole group. The participant might have been able to see that it was not the moderator or any other single person in the group who decided what would be discussed and worked on, but instead it was a group decision.

One member of the iCom team reflects:
"After a slight hesitation – should we try it? – we negotiated the roles, arranged the chairs to avoid obstacles, and started. Very early in the role-play it became apparent to me that the 'insisting participant' really came with expectations. She wanted these to be fulfilled and pushed for this. The moderator made it pretty clear that the key theme, however, was different."

> **Invitation to reflect**
> - Do the team findings resonate with you?
> - What seems still unresolved in your thinking about dealing with a demanding teammate?
> - What else would have been interesting to track?
> - Is role-play an option for you to find out about interpersonal conflicts in a business workplace?

Insights

During the role-play various learnings occurred, among them:
- There were less negative emotions towards the insisting participant due to better understanding of her situation.
- The team developed ideas about how this participant could be received without exactly following her goals.
- Role-play in our team can be fun and a rich source of learning.

Case 3:
Do YOU have a support group?

Keywords: Group, personal vision, dialogue.

Situation
A one-week workshop of the La Jolla Program organized by the Center of Studies of the Person was coming to an end. One of the facilitators, Peter, expressed his gratitude to his colleagues, and Renate joined the dialogue.

Scenario
P: Peter   *R:* Renate

P: "I'm so grateful I can be on the staff of this workshop. We can share our concerns during the whole year and in particular in the preparation of the workshop."

R: "Sounds wonderful, Peter, I appreciate to hear this and can imagine it's nice to be a part of such a facilitator team. As a participant here I felt you complemented one another really well, and this was a pleasant experience for me in this workshop."

P: "Oh, thanks, Renate! (pause) I'm curious whether you have such a group of people around you in Vienna with whom you can freely share and be there for each other emotionally."

R: (As a first reaction a complaint came to my mind because I didn't have such a group. But something surprising happened as I heard myself responding.) "Well, not exactly at the moment, but I know a few persons with whom we could initiate such a group." (This felt a lot more positive, and I knew what I would be up to once I got back to Vienna.)

Comment
Renate: "This experience that was born of such a small co-incidence in the workshop had and still is having such a powerful impact on me – it's hard to believe. The open and empathic workshop atmosphere must have influenced me so strongly that within a few seconds my inner and expressed response changed so decisively. Moreover, what I expressed in my own words in front of a group of about 30 people turned a silent intention to a powerful tendency to act."

> **Invitation to reflect**
> - Do you have a team, or group to facilitate your development, task completion, and innovativeness? If not, build one.
> - What groups are you or could you be a part of that could function more like a team?

Case 4:
When informal works well...

Keywords: Meeting, informal, exchange of experience, sharing, reflection.

Situation
From time to time, a handful of computer science and management teachers met to share their experiences, problems and questions regarding teaching and researching into teaching practice in the course of the iCom project. We trusted each other fully and were curious about the others' experiences and opinions. Time was always short, but we looked forward to the next meeting. The idea emerged to organize a bigger group in order to let more colleagues benefit from our sharing and to increase our perspective by the viewpoints of new teachers. But how could we attract new teachers to join us?

Scenario
We produced an agenda that gave some minimal structure to the event, so that much freedom for sharing whatever came to one's mind was preserved but at the same time there would be some orientation, in particular for new participants. Furthermore, two facilitators were appointed and an invitation letter was sent out. In fact, we succeeded to organize a group and attracted some new teachers to join us. While the meeting was quite productive, it was not as much of a significant, pleasant, immediate and spontaneous learning experience as the totally informal, small gatherings had been. In our reflection we arrived at the following hypothesis: If informal meetings work well, imposing structure and formalities and jumping to a larger frame does not necessarily mean a jump forward. Some qualities simply seem not to scale upward, so we even more appreciate them the way they are.

Comment
Interestingly, the way we continued with the teacher encounters took a form that combined the totally informal character with one that included a somewhat larger circle of colleagues and written invitation. Furthermore, the "network" or better community is alive by collaborating and meeting on multiple occasions and in various forms.

> **Invitation to reflect**
> - Do you share your experience with others? Do you prefer one person, a very small, or a larger group to share your experience?
> - Do you think that informal meetings could help in your work context to enhance experience-based learning among your team members?
> - When does it make sense to open a small circle to more people?
> - What is it that formal procedures tend to extinguish and how can those effects be minimized?

Insights
- Each setting has unique features.
- Smaller and larger groups have complementary benefits and drawbacks.
- The environment and in particular the process initiating a meeting tend to have a significant influence on a meeting.

Potential strategies
Think about various forms of sharing experience with colleagues/friends and try to find out which settings/surroundings you prefer. Is there also a benefit for your relationship/s and/or the organization? If so, can you describe it?

Don't let enriching contacts and ideas be swallowed by formalities and formal requirements.

Case 5:
Schools can help develop team skills

In the first iCom Practice-Research Workshop with participants from ICT-companies, a business partner complained that the first thing they had to teach new employees coming from school or higher education institutions was to re-learn engaging in issues of personal significance. Hereby, it can be considered highly important to work together in a group of people since most ICT-endeavors are worked on in teams. How can schools support students in finding out about how they can best work together with others?

Keywords: Skill development, teamwork, pair programming, significant learning, learning by experience, project.

Situation
Even though a mix of methods is important to diversify lessons or developmental initiatives, students' and workers' work in small groups is important for developing skills to work together in teams. This example suggests how such learnings can take place in practice.

Scenario
Teamwork in computer science is best suitable if participants work on a task on the computer. A group of students, rather than only one or two, carry out demounting a computer in its parts for learning how a computer works.

Students then can collaboratively make presentations about how a computer works in taking pictures of the parts and combine it with information about it that can be provided on a learning platform or researched by the students themselves.

Comment
One of the iCom team members who is teacher at a secondary school, shares:
"I have, for example, made very positive experiences with pair programming in my computer science classes, where several students work together in developing an application. Here it is often the case that different interests of pupils surface. Some are technicians, others like to organize, and others like to solve problems. This variety of competencies can be an advantage in pair programming. Everybody can contribute with something to the group

to create a product collaboratively. Students learn primarily to value their personal strengths and to cooperate in a team. This means, that they learn to use and combine their strengths and the strengths of their teammates to get the best out of the collaborative endeavor."

What students say about the teamwork:
- "Everyone should work in a team, the work needs to be split well. And teammates should help one another or they should get along well with each other and have fun at work."
- "Good teamwork is when all in the group get along well with each other and when everybody finishes work on time. Team members should stick together, talk with each other and work together."
- "Nice collaboration, just split work, help and support each member."

> **Invitation to reflect**
> - Do you see a connection to project teams in business environments?
> - What, in your view, could be done to improve team members' collaboration?
> - What opportunities for teamwork would you introduce at school or work?

Case 6:
Loneliness on the top

Keywords: Listening, empathic understanding, upper management.

Situation
On a recruiting fare, Renate is in contact with managers to find out about their communication habits:

R: Renate   *M*: top manager
R: "Well, what about you: Do you have someone to listen to you?"
M: "No, (pause) not any more in my position … "

Comment
Many people on the top complain that they have no one to share with, no one who would listen to their problems. Isn't there a chance to listen and learn from such persons, once you convince them you're really interested in their experience? Vice versa, sharing power and influence with the team can transform the loneliness into an experience of shared problem solving.

Interestingly, at universities top professors appear to hold their keynotes first in their research groups!

Our insights

The cases show that receiving different perspectives and learning in a team are unique opportunities for gaining new experiences and knowledge. In Case 2, Anne got the opportunity to take another person's perspective in a role-play – this setting would not have been possible without her team. Having a group or team for sharing your own experience and receive others' perspectives enables deep learning (Case 3). Such groups do not need to be formalized. Case 5 illustrates that informal sharing enables even more significant learning. Both the manager and the team can benefit from sharing to reduce loneliness and improve problem solving, but only if trust can be built in both directions through excellence in listening (Case 6).

Next steps to competencies

Do the following ideas make sense to you?

- Organization
  - When you provide space for communication among co-workers in your organization, it can help to share the knowledge naturally and to sustain relationships.
  - Be very careful when choosing the team leaders and team members. It is ideal when all of them get along well.
  - And last but not least, enable flexible work structures for teams to unfold (see topic: "*Hold constructs flexibly*").

- Team
  - When solving a problem, it can be valuable to engage all participants in the dialogue. Try to tap the experience of team members to get broad insights on an issue. This can lead to a very creative solution. However, it can also lead to frustration when some participants consider the problem to be unimportant or too easy so be judicious in the offering of full dialogue.
  - When training team members to sense into various situations, you may try out role-play or other group techniques.
  - When meetings and discussions are held in a rather threat-free interpersonal climate, this may strengthen sharing of experience (see topic: "*Care for the atmosphere*").

- Individual
  - On finding ones' place in a group:
    Standing and breathing – respect others' quirks and strengths and care for oneself.
    Taking a step – differentiate and share the personal experience (value ones' own perception, be aware of assumptions and feelings, test personal hypotheses about others and situations).
    Trying to walk in the others' shoes – build sensitivity for others' perspectives and feelings (consider herefore: Active Listening Exercise).
    Dancing – sense into work challenges, engage in personally worthwhile work situations and express yourself.

Final reflections

In what ways do you agree with the following statement?
- If you want to be fast, go alone; if you want to get far, take a friend.

Transparency yields flow

In work situations it is vital how and which information is communicated towards whom.

We can observe **transparency** on different levels:
- **On a personal level, this signifies that experiences and associated feelings are available to awareness, can be clearly named, and can be shared with others, if perceived appropriately**.
- **In a project team, transparency refers to sharing project-relevant information openly.**
- **In an organization, transparency means that information can easily pass position- and department-borders if necessary.**

Accessible forms of supporting transparency are, for example, short statements on work progress in meetings or some sort of information radiator like a flipchart in the office showing important information for the team, a Kanban board, a wiki or a versioning system (Elssamadisy & West, 2006).

What is the value of transparency at work? **Being transparent in business can help to increase productivity and customer relationships.** Having information transparently available for everybody at any time within an organization reduces risks of bottlenecks and inefficiency. Working hours can be spent productively if important information can be retrieved easily. With regards to communication with the customer, it can be helpful to share information on progress, motivation, expectations and actively involving customers from the beginning. These practices help to regularly check if the customer's expectations are continually understood and improve personal as well as informal relationships with the customer.

If information can flow freely, this may be connected with a feeling of ease to pursue the things that truly inspire or are relevant to us (Csikszentmihalyi, 2009). Flow leads to optimal experiencing, both for innovativeness and personal satisfaction. We can draw from many resources in addressing work and life challenges when information exchange can be transparent.

Given we aim for flow, and transparency yields it, how can we motivate and achieve transparency? How can I as a manager create and cultivate a climate in which the most appropriate level of transparency prevails? Is there anything I can do to challenge or counteract excessive hiding or playing roles?

Keywords: Processes, collaboration, (work) flexibility, transparency, conflict, flow, team, openness, clarity, motivation.

Cases

Overview of cases

The first three cases outlined illustrate the potential of transparently sharing in organizational and project team contexts. Further, effects of work situations that lack transparent communication can be grasped. The last case describes a setting for problem solving in small groups that supports transparent, open sharing.

- Case 1 **"Moving forward with work process transparency"** demonstrates a decline in motivation in a project team due to a lack of transparent change processes in higher management.
- Case 2 **"Reveal personal interests as soon as possible"** describes from the perspective of the project team leader how a co-worker in a project team engaged in work after having the opportunity to state his expectations.
- Case 3 **"Budget allocation"** describes the blocking effect non-transparent communication of valuable information, such as budget issues, might have on employees.
- Case 4 **"Exploration of experience in work contexts by "Open Case""** gives an insight into a setting for collaborative problem solving in a business environment that highly encourages transparent, open sharing of participants.

Case 1:
Moving forward with work process transparency

Keywords: Processes, business process management, collaboration, work flexibility, transparency.

Situation

During a commercial project, a very open agile team was formed. The customer was involved in the development and, to squeeze out the maximum out of the team agility, all developers were present during every meeting with the customer and also at meetings with the higher management of the organization (see also topic: *"Connect the dots"*). The initial performance of the development team was great and beat the expectations of stakeholders significantly.

Initially the agile, open team setting was perceived as perfect and the team performed very well, the customer and higher management were immediately informed about the progress in development, developers received feedback from the customer immediately. The whole process was highly transparent; everybody in the team was informed about the decisions and plans of higher management of the organization. However, things took a turn for the worse.

Scenario
The involvement of each participant in the project raised the motivation of the development team, as they felt strongly involved even in managerial decision-making, which is not very common in ICT-development. In short, at the beginning of the project, the overall project transparency was very high.

However at a certain point there were some issues at the very top of the management hierarchy in the organization, which led to personal changes among people supervising the project. Due to the turbulent situation such a change happened again in a very short period of time.

Despite the fact that people who were replaced were just supervising the project and their replacement did not have any direct impact on the development process, the secondary impact was very destructive. The situation got unclear; gossip about the reasons for the changes in the management appeared soon. The whole situation was not transparent anymore, and developers started to worry about the future of the project and felt insecure. Furthermore it led to conflicts in the team as some people had information (even though those maybe were just rumours) and the others did not; the trust among team members was lost. Finally, about half of the team members left the team and the initial perfect agile collaboration was gone.

Comment
The situation changed very rapidly and everybody was surprised how it ended up. Even some of the people who were leaving the team realized that there was no actual problem on the development level. However, the loss of trust in the team and also the management was perceived as the key to the problems in agile collaboration.

Invitation to reflect
- Should the whole process be transparent to everybody (team member/team leader)?
- Should the big picture be public? What information should not be public?
- How do you deal with the situation when turbulence in transparency results in loss of trust among team members? Can such a process be reversed?

Insights
Transparency can be very helpful to foster commitment, teamwork and trust among people.

Even a small decrease of transparency can have very destructive consequences, particularly if it occurs rapidly and/or from upper management.

Many ICT-professionals perceive it as pleasant to work highly transparent in teams; however we have to be sure we are able to maintain a high level of transparency all the time. Once people get used to it, they will be very sensitive to any step down from that level.

Potential strategies
As a manager, keep the transparency at the highest level at which you feel safe and at which you are able to maintain it in the long-term.

Try to identify team members struggling because of lack of information and provide opportunities to share information.

Case 2:
Reveal personal interests as soon as possible

Keywords: Transparency, communication, conflict, flow, synergy, team, dialogue, openness, flexibility.

Situation
In an ICT-project, a "senior" colleague leaves the project. A young project member is supposed to take the position of the senior person in the team. Project participants have no idea that the "junior" person is not prepared to undertake the role of the leader of a particular project part.

Scenario
The team leader in the project illustrates: "One (crucial) part of our project was led by one of my colleagues (let's call him senior researcher). He was very thoughtful and hardworking and in that time the project evolved very well. Most of the time he was working alone but later he started to cooperate with another colleague who joined the project as a junior researcher. After two years of their collaboration, the senior researcher finished his studies and left the project. So, for me, it was natural that the 'junior' should undertake the responsibility for their part of the project, and I automatically assumed that. And in this phase I made a huge mistake – I didn't

discuss the new situation with the 'junior' at all. So I missed the chance to reveal that he is not very comfortable in his new role. Then it took more than one year to make the situation clear (many speculations and discussions) and in consequence this part of the project slowed down in that period.

When we clarified the situation and reorganized the team structure and responsibilities, the 'junior' started to cooperate and enjoy working on the project – just because we changed his responsibilities and he wasn't 'forced' to lead and control other persons on the project. He simply loves working on his own, and we didn't learn it in time."

Comment

The project manager reflected on her perception of that situation: "At the first moment, I was quite confused and didn't understand what was wrong. From annoying moments I slowly revealed where the problem is, but it took too much time. My mistake was obvious – when the situation in the team changed, I shouldn't have assumed anything and should have discussed the needs and interests of the team members immediately.

Now I'm trying to discuss with colleagues and to be more mindful of their abilities and needs. And I don't assume anything. It's better to ask twice than never – it helps to avoid many problems in the future."

Invitation to reflect
- What would you have done in the position of the project manager?
- In your work context, is it easy to voice feelings about responsibilities and work situations?

Insights

Enabling opportunities to share feelings and considerations about work situations gives insight into team members' motivation.

Active listening and dialogue may support grasping what team members are up to.

Case 3:
Budget allocation

Keywords: Transparency, vagueness, clarity.

Situation
For special achievements, an organizational unit got a bonus payment. However, it was not clear if this budget needs to be consumed within one year or could have been transferred to the next year. While this situation may sound very simple, in fact it was not, and the unclear situation cost mental resources by creating a constant loop of considerations on how the budget could have been spent if this was necessary not to lose it.

Scenario
An international expert was invited to give a presentation and workshop at the unit but couldn't come. Additionally, due to a new project, time resources got so tight that nobody from the unit would participate in an international conference abroad that year.

An employee reflected: "But what will happen with this year's bonus? Can it be transferred to the following year? Should the boss be asked? Sure, but doesn't this expose that the unit has too many resources such that next year less money could be allocated? Isn't there something we could buy in December that would help us? But inviting the expert for next year would have clear priority. So should he be asked whether he'd like to come later? But what if the budget can't be transferred?"

Considerations like these consumed lots of mental resources that could have been spent a lot more productively if it just was clear that budget can be transferred.

The employee reflected again. "So – ask the boss and explain the situation. I'm sure he'll understand it. Organizational habits are that such requests are best sent by email. So I will sit down and explain everything clearly and send a clear request to the boss." But the employee waited and waited. She began to wonder, why is there no response till the turn of the year? Perhaps the boss's situation is a similar one?

Then the happy resolution – An email around the turn of the year says it black and white: Bonus payments can be transferred to the next year! What a nice relief …

Comment

A clear reaction is: "Next year this won't happen to me again – but quite regularly it does happen year by year, in particular, if the budget is tight and you are a person who wants to 'play it safe' and wants to have some options open for exciting opportunities."

> ### Invitation to reflect
> - Have you experienced a similar situation in which lacking a response from another party has blocked you in your work?
> - How did you feel and react?
> - How would you react as the boss?

Insights

Unclear situations bind mental resources. Such loops tend to block goal-directed activities. Once a decision is made, a stream of relief flows through body and mind. Such relief can help to focus on work activities again (see also topic: *"Hiding consumes energy: Untie and focus"*).

Potential strategies

It may be helpful to figure out the worst case and see if one is prepared to accept to live with the uncertainty and just go ahead with other activities.

Having as many factors as possible transparent and trusting the boss can help to minimize the mental loops. A quasi-decision is simulated, and the loop can (almost) be stopped.

Case 4:
Exploration of experience in work contexts by "Open Case"

"Time is going so fast. My mind is in a 'flow'. I feel that all of us are interested and feel valuable."
Description of an Open Case session by a participant at an iCom Practice-Research Workshop

Keywords: Openness, transparency, flow, motivation, complexity, interest, community, unconditional positive regard.

Situation
In iCom Practice-Research Workshops various settings were experimented with that enabled open sharing of experiences between people from industry and academia concerning challenging work situations (see also topic: *"Knowledge grows from sharing"*). One setting that appeared to be particularly worthwhile was labelled "Open Case" by members of the iCom team. The main purpose of "Open Case" is to provide a platform to share and explore experiences concerning business and life challenges in a rather open, constructive communication climate in a small group (Haselberger & Motschnig, 2013). It is a collaborative attempt to sense into a common field of interest (Senge, 2006). Personal viewpoints, feelings and meanings can be shared and reflected in dialogue (Isaacs, 1999). "Open Case" sessions are typically facilitated by a person experienced in the field that lives personal values such as authenticity and unconditional positive regard. The facilitator tries to empathically understand participants in the session. According to studies stemming from the Person-Centered Approach and common factor research in psychotherapy, these attitudes are essential to helpful relationships (Rogers, 1957; Lambert and Ogles, 2004).

In such an "Open Case" session at the Practice-Research Workshop in Vienna, a workshop participant shared a challenge of immediate personal relevance in his work life. He took the opportunity to reach towards a solution with experts in the field, consultants, affiliates of universities and project managers in a small group of about six people.

As a project manager and agile team leader in an IT company, he was considering the people and roles in self-organized teams. His concern stemmed from a situation where some programmers in a team of the company developed a feature that was not highly advertised by salesmen nor really needed by most customers as he found out later. As it turned out, one customer wished for the feature talked to an influential marketing person in the company who again talked directly to some programmers who didn't see the larger picture, stopped working on the task they were after, and integrated the feature that they were asked for. He was wondering whether people from marketing, direct customers, or salesmen may be part of the development teams. During the "Open Case" session, several forces in his organizational context contributing to the problem could be discerned, including that the agile approach development teams utilize is backed by the CEO, but nevertheless handled as a black box in the company. Thus, the idea of agile management was not present in other departments apart from development. A "push or pull" marketing strategy was discussed. A participant asked, whether it was the company that knew what customers need and "push" their product on the market, or whether customers may be approached for feature considerations of the software, such that the features are "pulled" into marketing. Furthermore, the group discussed communication channels with the CEO that frequently brought in new ideas to the development teams and changed requests he wanted to see implemented that may take precedence over what people worked on.

In reflection sheets by the participants in this group, the session was described as open, inspirational, and helpful to the entire group.

Scenario

To demonstrate more vividly the process in the "Open Case" session, we present an excerpt of the conversation which explored what to consider when building a self-organized team. The vignette is accompanied by short notes and interpretations about the process in the session from an outside perspective and from a person of the group.

The "Open Case" sessions at the Practice-Research Workshop were split in two parts with a break and a short scientific presentation in between. The excerpt is from the beginning of the second part of the session. The original session transcript was shortened and slightly edited for readability. Peter is the one who shared his problem and others are responding.

Second part of the open case session:

Jim, Mike, Peter, Louis, Alex & Rose (team members)

Jim: "I was just thinking about compatibility issues. If you are working agilely on the development side, what structure fits on the business side to it? (see topic: *"Maximize the chance for success: Be agile"*)."

Mike: "I also understand your question or comment like this: That you have agile inside development, but what about the other organization units – like, it should affect all the organization, but it doesn't probably?"

Peter: "Sure, what is closely related to the structure that I mentioned before or in the beginning was: Yes, we should get the agile or Scrum or whatever we call it company-wide. We should get the product marketing guy or, I don't know how to call that position, let's say, someone closer to promoting the product to the team. Or this technical guy maybe knows about code, maybe knows how many customers asked for this technical feature. But I know if he is able to get back to the market and promote and, I don't know how to, share the visibility of the new things developed."

> Commentator 1: Following Jim's contribution, Mike phrases his perception on the organizational problem introduced by Peter. Peter feels understood by Mike and picks up on his paraphrasings by exploring his wishes and possible solution strategies.

Louis: "There is something I would like to say. First is this: What do you think of the CEO, his visions? What influences him to come up with such visions?"

Peter: "Mhm, great question."

> Commentator 1: Louis shares his curiosity on what influences Peter's boss to develop his change requests. Peter declares his surprise.

> Commentator 2: In my view, Peter agrees that this is worth being considered.

> Commentator 1: The question offers a way to explore forces that influence decisions of Peter's boss and could help the understanding of his bosses' decisions, thus bringing deeper understanding of the relationship to his boss and environmental circumstances affecting it. After two seconds of silence in the group, Louis continues.

Louis: "So, secondly from my experience from where I worked before, a larger company with possibly more than 200 people, there are times with meetings of many people, and there are departments who still have a lot of information hidden. When heads of the company find out, they come and show the direction. So it is necessary to prepare peoples' minds, how an issue can be handled. So, if such information is also in your company, in search for a social direction, it will also help people, and also the CEO, to understand about the urgency of change and to increase the acceptance of the change through modelling."

> Commentator 1: From personal experience, Louis shares that he perceived it to be necessary that role models in leading positions live the social direction, interpersonal skills and personal attitudes they want to see in the organization. He affirms the efforts of Peter to care for opening up information exchange between departments in his company.

Alex: "There is one aspect that crossed my mind: You are lucky that you have a very good CEO, a visionary, like, when this guy talks everybody listens. But if you have an organization where you have a CEO, and most people in the organization believe that this guy is not competent then you can put them in one room, and it doesn't help."

Mike: "Yeah. It doesn't work."

Alex: "We have to keep this in mind. This guy has to be a good leader, model what he wants, and talk from the position of authority, otherwise…"

Mike: "It is contraindicated (laughs)…"

Alex: "…This whole structure doesn't make any sense." (laughs)

Peter: "You know, you are absolutely right, but sometimes, when he overwrites what was being done, you have to trust him, just trust him and say: Okay, that is your idea, I am going to develop it. But sometimes you are not able to own that, to really – you know, it is not my idea, I am going to develop it for him, but – yeeeah…"

> Commentator 1: Alex reminds Peter to feel lucky for having a visionary CEO that people in the organization listen to. Mike and Alex accord that good, sometimes authoritative leadership is essential for a well-functioning organization. While agreeing to the necessity of a good leader, animated through the indirect defence and praise of Peter's bosses' position of authority, Peter elaborates on his dissatisfaction with decisions of his boss in his team.

Rose: "I was wondering whether that is not frustrating for the team if they work on something a long time and then the boss says, "No, we need to do it this way.""

> Commentator 1: Rose is trying to empathically shape in her words what she understood of Peter's statement. She particularly focuses on a feeling aspect by offering her puzzling about frustration in the development team.

Peter: "You know, the situation was…"

Rose: "Just throw it all away?"

Peter: "Mhm, yes, it was, but it was just, let's say, two weeks, so it was not fully developed. It was just a little bit of research. So that is the good thing, that we just did some short estimates, like…"

> Commentator 1: Peter is quickly responding to Rose's reaction, explaining why frustration was actually minimal.

Rose: "So, it was caught it in the early phase, when there is not such a strong identification…"

Commentator 1: Rose differentiates her perception and paraphrases in her own words Peter's expression. Also, an interpretation from a leadership perspective is offered on why frustration was rather minimal.

Peter: "Yeah, right. And he said, "No, I don't like that, and we are going to change it." So there was nothing developed, just, let's say, a prototype that was done in two or three hours."

Commentator 1: Peter accepts Rose's paraphrase and illucidates how changes are handled in his team by imitating a slightly exaggerated direct speech of his boss. Then he reassures her that his frustration was minimal as only a small prototype, got developed.

Rose: "Still might be frustrating, but not so frustrating in this case."

Peter: "Yeah, where to begin?"

Commentator 1: Rose is trying to adjust her understanding of what Peter shared of the team situation by lessening her evaluation of the level of frustration that was present.

Commentator 2: The excerpt confirmed my impression that the setting can be exhausting to the case provider since he/she is typically asked several questions and hinted to several directions and ideas. Personally, I remember quite well the open case sessions in which I participated so far and also, that giving hints from own experience seemed to be helpful but to a limited degree, in a sense: Yes, that's an important issue/interesting aspect/should be considered, I could try, … however often the hints didn't seem to fit the case provided immediately as something like "Yes, that's it, that is the point, this is what I have to do …".

Comment

Attributes participants of "Open Case" sessions used to describe the setting:

- Accepting, open, creative, supportive.

- Inspiring, open-minded, interesting setting.

- Providing open discussion, new points of view for me, finding out that cultural change is sometimes hard to surmount.

- Cooperative, solution providing, consulting.

- Slowly developing into something quite interesting, enlightening.

- Interesting, complex, entangled, well-known, familiar, opening up new perspectives, creating confidence.

- Close, dynamic, open, nice.

- Good open discussion, exchange of experience, open-minded colleagues.

Invitation to reflect
- After reading the transcript, how would you feel in the position of the case provider?
- Would the open case setting, talking openly with like-minded people, support you in your endeavors?

Insights

Workshop structures that enable free sharing on issues of personal relevance open up space for collaborative problem exploration.

Persons presenting a personal issue in a rather short timeframe may gain from empathic group moderation.

Hints and suggestions may not always have the same value as personal discovery in empathy, but may point to or help integrate important perspectives.

Potential strategies

A guideline for the implementation of the "Open Case" method can be found at www.icomproject.eu/press/downloads/open_case_guideline.pdf.

Our insights

Presumably not by chance many modern ICT-project practices describe transparency as one of the most important aspects of working together.

Transparency in project teams eases decision-making through having important information immediately available. Moreover, team members can attune to each other as they get to know of others' progress and challenges. This can be a source of motivation in the team.

In interpersonal relationships, transparency enables trust. Not knowing the state of affairs can be demotivating and consume lots of energy. Where do I stand? If I don't know, how can I move on effectively? (See also the topic *"Hiding consumes energy: Untie and focus"*.)

Particular settings facilitate open sharing of experiences in a work context, may it be sitting in the kitchen with other team members during coffee break or a workshop that enables participants to bring their personal challenges to a dialogue with other experts in similar areas. "Open Case" is a practical opportunity to enable such sharing in a business environment.

Next steps to competencies

Do some of the following ideas make sense to you?

• Organization 　– Think out of the box! Create a climate of openness where bridging the gap between research and practice is possible.
• Team 　– Provide opportunities for open exchange of experiences. Make decisions and work steps transparent to team members and other contributors. Use information radiators such as status boards, flipcharts, posters.
• Individual 　– Differentiate meaning (in dialogue with somebody else). Label feelings. Share experience, when perceived appropriate.

Final reflections

In what ways do you agree with these statements?
- Transparency is risky – but brings deep insight.
- Transparency brings serenity.
- Transparency increases visibility and invites discussion, dialogue, encounter.
- Transparency encourages conflict that can be resolved rather than conflict that erodes trust and motivation.

References

Csikszentmihalyi, M. (2009). *Flow*. New York: HarperCollins.
Elssamadisy, A., & West, D. (2006). *Adopting Agile Practices: An Incipient Pattern Language* (pp. 1–10). Presented at the PloP 2006.
Haselberger, D., & Motschnig, R. (2013). *Dealing with change in a complex environment from a person-centered, systemic perspective*. IPMA conference (submitted for publication).
Isaacs, W. (1999). *Dialogue: The Art Of Thinking Together*. New York: Currency.
Lambert, M. J., & Ogles, B. M. (2004). The efficacy and effectiveness of psychotherapy. In: M. J. Lambert (Ed.), *Bergin and Garfield's handbook of psychotherapy and behavior change* (5 ed., pp. 139–193). New York: Wiley.
Rogers, C. R. (1957). The Necessary and Sufficient Conditions of Therapeutic Personality Change. In: *Journal of Consulting Psychology, 21*, 95–103.
Senge, P. M. (2006). *The fifth discipline: the art and practice of the learning organization/Peter M. Senge*. London/Sydney: Random House.

Further resources:
Open Case Guideline, a generic guideline to the process of the Open Case setting:
www.icomproject.eu/press/downloads/open_case_guideline.pdf

Open Case Reflection Sheet:
www.icomproject.eu/press/downloads/open_case_reflection_sheet.pdf

Leadership

Hold constructs flexibly

Constructs appear in several forms: established policies, specifications of how work is to be done (i.e., planning), how organizations should be structured, or what communication should look like.

We'd like to illustrate what it means to 'hold constructs flexibly'. This does not mean chaos or laissez-faire leadership, and it does not mean rigidity or autocracy. It means to decide, moment-by-moment, if the structures, plans, regulations, and practices are adequate to reach one's objective and then to act accordingly. Having plans and structures is necessary. They provide a feeling of security, something to hold on to: be it a habit, familiar situation, expectation, or contract. Still, a plan or structure must not necessarily mean a strict rule or inevitable procedure. In some work situations, it might be necessary or enhancing to work around rules and structures, see things from different perspectives, and adapt to quick internal and external changes.

What are constructs? Constructs are ubiquitous in our thinking. We inevitably build schemas to make our thinking more effective, as suggested by Jean Piaget. Whenever information arrives, we try to match it with existing schemas to find a personally proven response and only when this process fails, we build a new schema. So while schemas (i.e., models, patterns, rules, habits, prejudices, emotional responses, etc.) tend to make our thought and behavior more effective, there are (new) situations in which they can block us unless we hold them flexibly. How can we encounter the challenge of harnessing constructs and yet not letting them take over and thus dominate our thinking, feeling, and behavior? In particular, what can we do if we aren't even aware of our constructs? The following cases might provide some inspiration.

Keywords: Authenticity, positive regard, learning from experience, sensing, listening, complex understanding, flexibility, planning, schema, process model, rule.

Cases

Overview of cases

The following six cases illustrate different contexts in which constructs are necessary and helpful. However, if these constructs, in the cases manifested as work-plan, schedule, rule, agenda, expectation, procedure, and term are all that matters in a particular situation the result tends to be compromised. In particular:

- Case 1 **"Agile activities in classical management – Can conflict be held within bounds"** shows how a bright new idea to develop a generic tool instead of adapting existing ones meets resistance in a traditional management environment.

- Case 2 **"Planning a team meeting with an international consultant"** shares various perspectives on "last minute changes". As in Case 1, the context of a project needed to be managed according to traditional management practice.

- Case 3 **"You must not run down the corridor!"**, as you can assume from the title, is borrowed from the school context. It aims to "cry for the need to let the other express himself or herself", far beyond the school context where it appears "as a pure culture".

- Case 4 **"Disappointed participant"** shares the effects of not completely meeting the (expressed) expectations of a workshop participant and aims to question whether to follow the agenda or give it up temporarily.

- Case 5 **"Defined processes can enable collaboration rather than inhibit flexibility"** argues that creating constructs where none exist may be helpful. At the same time it illustrates the fear that people may have in explicating their lived and often loved practice.

- Finally, Case 6 **"Deadline – "dead"-line: Is there more than one in one's lifetime?"** critically deals with a term that became so common that we don't think about it anymore. It aims to motivate readers to become more sensitive to the way we use our language and what it imposes on us.

Case 1:
Agile activities in classical management – Can conflict be held within bounds?

Keywords: Work breakdown structure, classical management, agile development, conflict.

Situation
An international project to build a web-portal with 8 partners has well-defined tasks. One of them is the analysis and adaptation of assistive open-source tools to be provided via the portal. This activity, however, yields a minimal number of suitable tools such that just adopting existing technology would render a portal with little innovative value. One partner, let's call him XAG, has a bright idea of developing a multi-purpose assistive tool with high innovative potential. XAG develops a prototype and a representative presents it at the next project review meeting.

Scenario
XAG develops a prototype and a representative presents it at the next project review meeting.
PCO: Project Coordinator   *XAG*: Representative of the partner XAG

PCO: "The next presentation is from XAG, and I'm curious how your work has been going since we haven't heard about it like we have from the others."

XAG: "Well, we were busy with the idea until the last minute. We could, of course, simply list some existing tools and produce tutorials, but this wouldn't help. Why should users come to our site, if they don't use the tools that have been around for quite a while? This is a dead end for our portal. The only thing that makes sense in the current situation is to develop a better, general-purpose tool that they might use for (almost) any website. This is what XAG has been eagerly producing and I brought a prototype to show you how it would work."

PCO: "Are you serious? Are you saying that you did not do *any* of the work you agreed to do? Furthermore, you claim that you spent more time than allocated to do none of the work you were supposed to do?"

XAG: "I'm not going to invest my work in an application that won't be used once the project is over. What you were about to produce has no business value at all. If you don't want to hear me, I'm not going to waste my time but rather produce something that has potential. Do you want to take a look now?"

Comment
Expectations to follow an established plan are not fulfilled. Frustration and lack of understanding is evident on both sides. Openness to integrate the expectations with the new facts is missing.

> **Invitation to reflect**
> - If you were a representative of the partner XAG, how would you deal with the situation?
> - If you were the Project Coordinator, how would you deal with the situation?
> - If you were one of the other partners in the project, what would you do in the review meeting once the conflict became apparent? Under what circumstances would you be open or closed to the development of the assistive tool?

Insights
A plan can become obsolete due to new findings and facts.

It is essential to communicate any deviations from a plan as soon as possible and not to act in isolation.

Potential strategies
If you are not convinced that some adverse strategy is being practiced, try to trust that the other side has some good reasons why they behave the way they do.

Ask for the intentions and try to see their point. Then, try to see if it might fit in with your (or the established) plans with some minor or even major adaptations.

Once you know the other's mindset you are more likely to be in a position to suggest solutions and to be listened to by the other, in turn.

Case 2:
Planning a team meeting with an international consultant

Keywords: Planning, organizing, sub-teams, change.

Situation
A scientific consultant was brought in to enhance the research progress of the project. The scientific leader of the project intended a one-day session with the consultant together with the entire project team followed by individual one to two hour sessions with the individual team members – from both project partners.

Scenario
Once sub-teams A and B agreed on a possible time-range for the consultation, a date was fixed together with the consultant and sub-team A, while sub-team B was informed about the dates. At that point, sub-team B did not mention any concerns with the dates and schedule.

Later in the process, sub-team A planned with sub-team B the details of the schedule. At that time it came out that team members from sub-team B could not attend the one-day session due to overlaps with other appointments. After several discussions within the sub-team A on how they should deal with this fact, they decided to change plans and switch the one-day session to another date.

From the scientific leader's point of view, this seemed a feasible solution, as all project partners were included. From the organizer's point of view, this change caused several other changes and meant a lot of additional effort and time. This was particularly the case because the strict project settings imposed by the rigid regulations on conducting interregional projects (such as iCom) obliged the organizer to plan far ahead and to document each step. Thus, in the organizer's view, changes in such stiff environments tend to be very stressful. In this particular case, even though the organizer would personally have preferred to be able to plan more flexibly, the situation required her to adapt to the given circumstances.

Comment
Finally, in the consultation there was some redundancy and issues had to be repeated due the re-scheduling of the team-session. Retrospectively the solution was not perfect. Nevertheless, the shared experience of meeting with a renowned international consultant together left a strong impression.

Afterthought: There could be a general commitment about priorities. Was the additional (strong) effort of the organizer worth satisfying the sub-team B's current (changed or not previously expressed) needs?

> **Invitation to reflect**
> - Do you understand the scientific leader's and organizer's perspectives?
> - How would you have reacted as the scientific leader and as the organizer of the project?
> - How would you have handled the situation? Why?

Insights
Certainly, a main force in this case is the uncertainty of planning in projects, but also insufficient communication between sub-teams A and B.

Another influence might be different cultural constructs of how, when, and how precise planning is done as the sub-teams are from different cultural regions.

Building real commitment has to be started early and optimally be a shared process, continually. This requires time and effort to keep in touch.

Potential strategies

Include all people involved at the beginning of the planning process and involve them in decision-making early. This may seem very time-consuming (which it actually will be in the planning phase), but saves time in the following phases, as changes will not occur so frequently. Still, this strategy is only possible if there is the opportunity and willingness to invest more time in that stage.

When planning an event engaging multiple sub-teams, sharing the changes and evolvements *continuously* during the time with *all* participants is better than relying on perfect internal communication within individual sub-teams.

Let go of the idea that planning is a fixed process without any uncertainties. Rather, try to stay flexible because you cannot be sure that everything will go as planned. This may make it easier to react to changes in the future.

Case 3:
You must not run down the corridor!

Keywords: Authority, acting from one's position, not listening, punishment, feelings.

Situation

During a break, a 12-year-old pupil is physically attacked by his classmates because he stopped them accidentally when tossing his pencil case around. He grabs his pencil case and runs away down the corridor towards the teachers' lounge to find protection if needed. To his surprise, the opposite happens. A teacher grasps his arm and shouts at him.

Scenario

T: Teacher   *P:* Pupil

T: "Hey! Are you crazy, running about like you are mad? Have you ever heard the rules of conduct in the school building?"

P: "Yes, sure, I'm sorry but I …"

T: "Stop your fancy story. It doesn't interest me at all. I caught you running inside. At your age you should be intelligent enough to know that running down the corridor is strictly forbidden."

P: "I know that but …"

T: "No 'buts'! I'll help you to remember. First, you'll write 100 times, 'I must not run on the corridor'. And then you'll bring me a handwritten copy of the school rules. By tomorrow!"

Comment

These are experiences children don't forget easily. Experiencing injustice and helplessness and brute use of power over them may seriously influence how children and adolescents perceive their (social) environments. If pupils are dealt like this, how can we expect that they won't take revenge in some way, once they in turn have power? Tunnel vision may empower its holder, but it will never let sunshine enlighten his or her heart.

Invitation to reflect

- Can you characterize the feelings that are evoked in the situation described above:
  - In the pupil?
  - In the teacher?
  - In yourself?
- Are these feelings familiar to you?
- Do you know any situation (except for acute danger) in which listening to the other is not indicated?
- How could the situation described above still be turned into a learning experience by an understanding parent or teacher, or in its generalized context by a manager or consultant?
- Do you know of any fixed constructs you hold in the context of your work? Why are they important to you?

Insights

No rule exists without exceptions. Each situation is unique. While this case is a rather special one, it can easily be extended to cover the broad range of phenomena where a person evaluates a situation from a single side imposing authority such as a project plan, a habit, a norm, an instruction, a scientific source, a guru, etc. and sticks to that evaluation while absolutely ignoring any other clues and senses. Another person feels shame or unfairness compounded with an earlier injustice or misunderstanding. The level of listening equals zero and the same applies to the level of empathic understanding. We ask – is this humane?

Potential strategies
Try to meet the other at eye level, both as fallible persons. This does not necessarily mean to give in, but it does mean to try to understand the other from their perspective.

Case 4:
Disappointed participant

Keywords: Rules, collaborations with external partners.

Situation
The iCom team was preparing an interactive workshop where participants would have a chance to engage in collaborative problem solving of real cases from their practice (e.g., how to manage the change from classical to agile development). They discussed the following procedure. In Brno and Vienna, respectively, three industry partners would be asked to think about a change case that they would briefly present during the workshop. In this way the iCom team wanted to make sure that some interesting cases were offered even if (other) industry partners could not find a case spontaneously at the workshop.

Scenario
At the workshop, right before the case-presentation session, an industry partner had a special request:

IP: Industry partner   *T1, T2*: Various iCom team members

IP: "I prepared a few slides to present my case. Could you please help me to upload them such that I can present them?"

T1: "Well, it isn't necessary to present your case with slides. This would take too long. You are supposed to present it orally. But let me check with my colleague."

T1 (to *T2*): "An industry partner wants to show slides. I guess this was not intended and he should try to present it orally. Otherwise we're going to loose too much time!"

T2 (to *IP*): "I see, you prepared slides – and now we've set up everything for oral presentations. Actually, we planned just one minute or so per case-proposer. Do you think you'll manage to introduce your case briefly orally? This would really help us. The introduction just serves for participants to choose which case they wish to work on."

IP: "I can try but it is complex and I'm not sure if all will understand it."

T2: "Well, participants will just choose which case to work on. Later in the small team, you'll have plenty of time to explain more, perhaps using your slides."

IP: "I'll do as you suggest. We'll see."

T2: "Thank you so much. I hope it will work out well. So let's start the presentations."

Comment

The situation was not resolved optimally. The small team who chose this industry partner's case took too long to understand it. The industry partner wrote in his feedback that it was a mistake not to introduce cases properly in the initial session. The small team also complained about the session format. Nevertheless, this was the only case proposer who was not happy with the process. In any case, the situation provided an opportunity for learning beyond the content presented.

> **Invitation to reflect**
> - How did the conversation resonate with you? Do you think that constructs were held too rigidly to not allow the industry partner to present slides? What would likely be your reaction to a participant having special wishes at the very last moment?
> - What could increase the probability that problems/misunderstandings like the one described could be avoided?

Insights

Expectations are important and not meeting them may have adverse effects.

This case provides the re-experiencing of an old wisdom: You can't make please everyone.

Potential strategies

Specify the most important rules (e.g., cases are presented orally in up to 1 minute) in a written document that is given to participants.

Keep the agenda flexible such as to be better able to accommodate special or unexpected events.

Try to upload the presentation anyway but clarify with the participant and potentially the whole audience that the time limit cannot be extended substantially.

Case 5:
Defined processes can enable collaboration rather than inhibit flexibility

Keywords: Processes, Business-Process Management (BPM), collaboration, work flexibility.

Situation
During a process analysis done at an ICT-department at one of our universities, we performed several process-mapping interviews. Some employees were not happy with the process analysis effort. They felt that the definition of formalized processes would result in restrictions, and they would be less efficient in their work.

Scenario
We had an unfriendly conversation over a process diagram, where two of these employees, representing departments A and B, were trying to express their viewpoints, explaining why such process codification would be inefficient. They were strongly convinced that the process codification would result in worse cooperation between their departments.

Both employees used as an example a part of the process where their departments exchange some documents. However, each of them had a completely different picture how the cooperation proceeded and how the documents were processed.

Later it became apparent that department A provides several inputs to department B, which in turn are not used by B at all, and instead, a similar document is later created by a worker from department B.

The initial argument about the necessity of a process model ended up with an agreement and consequent simplification of the process. This simplification shortened the average process duration in half. Later the process model was created according to the suggestions of participants, and both of them accepted it.

Comment
Both of the participants came to the meeting with a goal of denial of any need for process codification. However during the discussion they started to express their own view of the process and as they could not agree, they forgot about their initial goal and started to insist on codification of their own version of the process.

Invitation to reflect
- Was the face-to-face discussion important for uncovering the problem?
- Could the same happen in series one-by-one interviews?
- Why could they not uncover the problem earlier during the work communication they have every day?

Insights
The discussions about process models can result in many proposals for a process optimization and improvements.

Discussion about the collaboration can uncover inefficiencies, even in very simple workflows.

Well managed conflicts tend to produce useful results.

Potential strategies
As a manager, provide employees with opportunities and incentives to talk about how collaborations are going and their potential improvement.

Try to map reoccurring processes at work and see whether there are uncertainties or redundancies.

Define processes as guidelines rather than rigid, inescapable regulations.

Any proposed change can cause resistance – come prepared.

Case 6:
Deadline or "Dead"-line: Is there more than one in one's lifetime?

Keywords: Deadline, stress, time and document management, use of language.

Situation
A deadline bears some magic within itself – things that don't get done for a long time suddenly get done, people work and consume their last supplies of energy. With firm deadlines all effort may be lost, or literally dies, if the deadline is not met. To alleviate things a little, the strange term "soft deadline" was created to provide some tolerance for those who are late – or to increase, for example, the number of submissions for the benefit of the organizers. All this raises the question: "Could timelines be organized more flexibly, with less stress but still promote efficiency?"

Scenario
Version 1: Training in project management
Instructor: The due date for assignment 1 is X. Given I manage to find time, I'm willing to accept your assignment 1 documents until Y but my feedback and evaluation may be delayed.

Teams who submit two assignments on time will be excused for one delayed assignment (up to five days late) without any effect on their grade.

Version 2: Submission of proposals
If you submit your proposal before X you may get feedback that you could use to improve your submission.

We confirm that proposals submitted until Y will receive full consideration.

Time permitting, late proposals submitted until Z will be considered, in particular, if their quality is estimated to be high. We can't guarantee, however, that such late proposals will enter the review process so be prepared to receive a note saying that your submission can't be handled because it missed the Y date.

Comment

You may be thinking: The airplane won't wait if you are late! – For sure there are events that need a fixed time. In the case of the airplane it is evident that the departure time needs to be fixed. On other occasions, however, our natural attitude towards time might be worth receiving more respect and be granted some flexibility.

Invitation to reflect
- How do you deal with due-dates or "deadlines" as the person who sets them?
- How do they feel as a "consumer" or one who must comply with them?
- Do you like "deadlines"?
- How do you deal with activities that are open in nature, not coming with a particular date on which they have to be done?
- Have you given proper thought to the advantages of time constraints?

Insights

As has been shown, there are options on how to avoid the word "deadline" so as to use language more sensitively. There also exist ways – and more wait to be invented – on how to manage time without the stress caused all too often by deadlines.

Potential strategies

Let the other person know. You can ask for an exception, but please respect that often requests arriving after the closing date can't be considered.

Ask the other party when they think they'll be ready.

Reveal more of the whole context such that timing and consequences of delays can be better understood.

State clearly if you won't accept items that are delayed.

Our insights

There's no doubt that constructs, schemas, rules, plans, guidelines, policies, and procedures make the majority of situations more efficient and thus need to be created, kept in place and propagated. These artificial constructs, however, should not substitute for and overrule common sense and basic human interactions. The world is too complex and too dynamic to be ever captured purely mechanically. In complex, open, dynamic systems new features and properties can emerge that lead to new ways of coping.

Next steps to competencies

Do the following ideas make sense to you for different levels of how to hold constructs flexibly?

- Organization
    - Promote and model listening to provide means for employees to share their perspectives such that they can loosen their rigidly held beliefs in a non-threatening atmosphere.
    - Help people save face and don't punish them when they change their mind or don't follow constructs, especially if they communicate this in timely and transparent manner.
    - Design for change rather than stability.

- Team
    - If in doubt, communicate.
    - Take potential changes into account whenever possible.

- Individual
    - Develop your listening skills and allow yourself to be changed by encounters with others. In other words, allow deep listening to others to facilitate you, not just others.
    - Learn from your experiences, notice when they are or can be new. If you are in a changing situation, reflect on what is going on in yourself and with others and why you acted like you did.
    - Know as many of your constructs as possible.

> - Make it your decision whether to follow a construct, or suspend or adapt it for some time.
> - Try new ways of doing old things to enrich your repertoire of experience.
> - Travel to other countries and meet people from different cultures and/or disciplines to widen your repertoire of constructs and adaptive dispositions.

Additional considerations to integrate the ideas

Consider the history of software development. Remember the waterfall model, and how once reflecting ultimate wisdom, it is no longer the only process in place.

For those who prefer a less technical example: Consider the history of the rules how to care for and feed babies. It is amazing how many errors were made, judging from the theories in place today. For example, feeding at fixed intervals gave place to feeding a baby when he/she is hungry.

Final reflections

In what ways do you agree with these statements?

- Acting outside of constructs demands courage and trust in oneself.
- Acting outside of constructs requires a special competence.
- What I know for sure that isn't necessarily so: Freedom is good, constructs are bad.
- Constructs provide something to hold on to, yet at the same time, constrain creativity.
- "There's nothing as practical as a good theory." (Kurt Lewin)

References

Stillwell, W., & Mooreman, J. (1998). *Conflict is inevitable. War is optional.* La Jolla, CA: Center for the Studies of the Person Press.

Care for the atmosphere

The influence of the atmosphere isn't necessarily conscious. However, **if you feel well, you will tend to be more open and your ideas will flow faster than if you feel tight, anxious, cold, hot, bored, etc. It does not matter if the atmosphere refers to physical atmosphere of a room or a building, or to the socio-psychological climate among persons in your team, class or meetings.**

In organizations, when the atmosphere is unpleasant, people tend to lose their motivation, fluctuation increases and projects or plans don't blossom, sometimes they even die. When nobody cares for the people, they simply do not feel like an integral part of the team. This, in turn, has a negative influence on relationships between team members and is likely to compromise their collaboration.

Especially when introducing changes – which influence some members or the whole team – it is important to put efforts into keeping the team atmosphere positive. **Being open to the worries that may burden a co-worker with a "willing ear" and honest concern for their issues will tend to be more helpful than leaning back and waiting for the unexpected. Being prepared and sensitive to the team atmosphere, change processes may be less "painful" and more successfully accepted by your team.**

Another fundamental part of the process in building a stable and "happy" team **is to establish a good mix of structure and freedom** (see also *"Hold constructs flexibly"*). Of course, employees have to be aware of basic norms and rules in the company. But revealing and unfolding potential by active listening to employee ideas and suggestions, and adopting the good ones strongly influences a shared feeling and sense of responsibility.

As a result, this leads to building more respect and trust within teams and increases team productivity.

Since a positive atmosphere seems to be a key success factor, questions such as the following seem worth asking:
- What contributes to the atmosphere and how is it influenced?
- What is different in a good or bad atmosphere? How do you realize this?
- What can a team leader do to improve or poison the atmosphere?

Keywords: Enabling potential, empowerment, motivation, sharing responsibility, academic-industrial cooperation.

Cases

Overview of cases

- Case 1 **"Turning an academic project into a commercial one"** describes problems and obstacles when transforming an academic project to a commercial product.

- Case 2 **"Personal learning time and knowledge exchange"** reflects experience with introducing free time for personal development to employees of the Kentico software company.

- Case 3 **"Masaryk University Science Park – Institutional knowledge transfer"** introduces you to a strategic development project fostering university-industry cooperation at Masaryk University and problems in attracting big multinational companies.

- Case 4 **"Atmosphere can enable openness"** advocates the importance of building a shared vision in the team or company.

Case 1:
Turning an academic project into a commercial one

Keywords: Spin-off, team, relationships, expectations, multiple perspectives, motivation.

Situation
A spin-off company from the Masaryk University, whose representatives attended several workshops of the iCom project, started as a group of researchers performing basic research at Masaryk University. After years of research on the academic level, scientists decided to transform a proved concept into a commercial product. They established a spin-off company but they had no experience with the business side. Moreover, the team was not prepared for changing their habits and starting to think and work "commercially".

Scenario
The beautiful idea of transforming an academic product into a commercial one followed by the establishment of a company was only the first step – the easiest one. Without any personal experience with marketing, the team concentrated on the development of the product and didn't realize the large efforts have to be made for introducing the product to the market.

Very soon this carried over to a problem in the team because the team members hardly accepted that the process of commercialization brings necessary changes in their methods of working. Developing a commercial product requires much faster implementation and adaptation to the needs of customers – and you have to deal with competitors. This approach tends to be very naturally accepted by team members when starting a company "from scratch". But for an already running academic project, it is very hard to convince the team members that it's time to change their work habits to develop a successful company.

As a result, processes which in a company usually take weeks prolonged to months. Some team members realized that changes were necessary; others did not realize or didn't want to admit it. Such situations naturally have a negative impact on the environment in the team and the project and business as well.

Comment
Commercialization definitely needs a business oriented person who is rarely a member of a research team. Therefore, it is almost necessary to hire such a person.

Team members are very enthusiastic about a project and the idea of commercialization, but they do not realize that it also brings big changes to their lives. The timelines for R&D are quick, and this is usually the opposite approach to what the team members experience at a university is like.

Invitation to reflect
- Have you ever experienced a similar situation?
- How would you solve this situation? Is it more effective to "teach" current team members to change their working habits? Or would you replace them with new developers who are experienced in working in for profit companies?
- Can you think of alternatives that would help in similar situations?

Insights
A mix of originators of the idea and newcomers with business experience is ideal. But this solution reveals another problem – what to do with the team members who are not able to adapt to a commercial environment and thus do not contribute anymore? Perhaps a strong and experienced team leader is needed to handle such situations?

Potential strategies
Short term: If the success of the project and the company is your main concern, make unpopular decisions and build a strong and highly productive team. Otherwise continue with the current team and patiently facilitate thinking and acting in the different manner.

Mid and long term: Make all consequences of the change you foresee transparent and ensure commitment and a shared vision of all team members upfront. This could be done, for example by inviting a team that has already undergone such a change and is willing to share their reflections.

In education: Use this case in the academic education of technicians to encourage and support them in getting both development and commercial skills. Allow students to decide themselves whether they want to concentrate on building their development or commercial skills, recognizing strengths and limitations of each.

Case 2:
Personal learning time and knowledge exchange

Keywords: Sharing responsibility, authenticity, learning together, co-actualization, multiple perspective, enabling potential, empowerment, inclusion.

Situation
In one of the Practice-Research Workshops organized by the iCom team it was mentioned that Kentico software grants free time for personal development to its employees. The iCom team found this an interesting idea and a good way to create a work climate in which self-initiated, self-organized learning and skill enhancement is appreciated.

The situation at Kentico is as follows: people who are starting to work at Kentico are quite young (on average 23 years). They are mainly looking forward to working for Kentico and being developers. They are skilled, have the knowledge, and love technology, but they do not have any experience from other companies or big projects. For such young people, specific leadership is needed.

Scenario

On a personal level, all the ICT-companies which are successful really care about their people, because it is very hard to get the right people. Those 'right' people are looking for independence to use their knowledge and develop ideas. And if they can accomplish that, they are happy.

Kentico is one such company, and the feedback from one of its project managers (PM) gave us an overview of how this is achieved in practice:

iCom: a team member from the iCom project   *PM*: project manager

iCom: "How does leadership at Kentico work?"

PM: "Our approach is based on coaching people to find their own way. Kentico does one-to-one meetings quarterly between their employees, team leaders and management. In these meetings, people just talk: how they like their work, what are their goals for the future, what projects in the past they really liked. Then, the team leader or manager is trying to coach the person to find his or her own way within Kentico. The management is really open to let people change within the company easily. For example, changing from developer to consultant with closer customer contact is usually possible. The company tries to give people the positions and tasks they really like to do."

Another initiative was to introduce what we called "innovation time" for our employees. It is based on the idea of giving people a certain amount of their time (20% of their employment) to do whatever they would like and whatever is really needed – without fear of failure, without processes, without asking for permission, without standardized rules. Also, people get feedback on what they are doing, but it is actually up to them what they do in this 20% time frame.

iCom: "Do employees actually take the time to develop new knowledge? How do they deal with discrepancies of stressful projects, meeting deadlines and taking 'free-development-time' off?"

PM: "It depends on the employees. Sometimes it is used when the developer recognizes a bad code which does not have any priority for the manager or product owner – then he can do the redesign in this time, if he really sees a value for further development, adaptations, or others. Or some people are interested in technologies which Kentico currently does not support but maybe in the future there will be the need to introduce them."

Of course, the amount of time spent on the 'innovation time' varies according to project deadlines in the given week or development cycle. Typically, these times did not lead to major innovations – but more importantly, people learned a lot in that free time. The most important is that people see a value in what they are doing and the free time gives them the opportunity to do things that are really valuable to them.

iCom: "How is the general acceptance of this approach by the employees?"

PM: "At the beginning, employees were afraid as they thought that they have to work more in total. But that was not a real threat. The management communicated, 'If you have problems with people that say that what you do in innovation time is not valuable or that you should not use the innovation time, come to me and I will communicate its importance and support you!' Currently new people get used to it quickly because now most people in the company use that free time."

iCom: "Did Kentico develop further practices of knowledge transfer?"

PM: "That is one point where there is still need for improvement – sharing ideas within the whole company. There is a wiki to share ideas. It's a challenge to share knowledge beyond teams within the company which shall be solved in the near future. In the teams, learning by working together is working well – Kentico is also trying Pair Programming (someone new paired with someone experienced) and both people in the pairs learn a lot there."

Comment

Kentico's culture allows people to know each other in person – this is highly encouraged by the management. It will not be that easy if the company grows, but the concept will remain: people and good cooperation are essential! Close relationships are necessary for a company to be coherent. That is also why the company finances team building time.

> **Invitation to reflect**
> - Do you think this approach can be adopted more generally?
> - Can you imagine introducing such an environment to your company?
> - Do you see obvious problems or possible improvements of the method taken by Kentico?

Insights
In such an environment, where people are encouraged to self-actualize and enabled to introduce their ideas, the "team spirit" is very strong. Of course, different people have different needs and habits. Kentico does not force the employees to adopt this system, it is just an option. And this is one of the strongest points of the whole idea – people can find their own level of "independence", and are consistently supported by the management.

Potential strategies
Listen to the needs of people you are working with. It can have two major consequences – their ideas, needs and suggestions can give you other views on the problems and help you to give the better directions to the project. Moreover, such atmosphere positively affects morale and the coherence of the team.

Case 3:
Masaryk University Science Park – Institutional knowledge transfer

Keywords: Care for the atmosphere, shared vision, academic-industrial co-operation, meeting at eye level.

Situation
CERIT Science Park is a strategic development project fostering ICT-related academic-industrial cooperations at Masaryk University by providing office spaces for ICT-companies in close proximity to the Faculty of Informatics. Though it looks like a 100% win-win opportunity for companies and the university, attracting the right companies to rent office rooms having the right size in a reasonable time is not an easy task, since the situation is very complex. There are many factors to take into consideration for all players.

Scenario
CERIT Science Park (CERIT-SP) builds upon a tradition of academic-industrial cooperation at the Faculty of Informatics. The purpose is to provide a common shared environment for companies and research teams from the Faculty of Informatics in close proximity to the university. PhD-students can act as both developers with innovative companies settled in the Science Park and at the same time do the research in collaboration with the rest of the team at the university – all in neighboring buildings. It will foster innovations in the companies, and bring interesting research problems back to the faculty. However, there are certain circumstances making the transformation of the vision into reality complicated. Let us examine this:

One (not rare) problem occurs when the industrial cooperation "goes beyond the horizon" of local companies. This occurs quite frequently because for many top-level research teams the big multinational companies are natural partners in large EU research projects while most of the local companies are left out. On the other hand, the local ones are more likely to join the Science Park for practical reasons – the park is not large enough to accommodate big companies. The big ones prefer to participate in R&D projects remotely, and in most cases the research team at the university is "just one of their research partners", not a reason to move the company there. Therefore, there are excellent teams at the university having a long tradition of industrial cooperation and still, they cannot attract any company to the park thus missing the opportunity of a convenient cooperation with them in the co-locality.

> **Invitation to reflect**
> - What sort of atmosphere was created within the MU Science Park?
> - What could have been motives of companies to move/not move there?
> - Do companies on campus collaborate closely with the university and with each other – or do they only use the office space there without connecting with each other?
> - What could be done to improve the collaboration?
> - How is the intensity of collaborations related to the atmosphere of the Science Park?

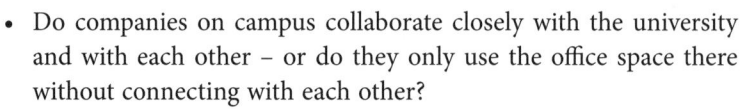

Insights

Co-location is just one out of several enabling factors (however important) for good collaboration.

For commercial institutions, *commercial factors* (naturally) tend to have priority. Taking this into account, shared visions including scientific and commercial facets need to be elaborated.

Companies have to see the real benefit of coming closer to the students and researchers.

Potential strategies

In our opinion, companies (as well as universities) can profit from
- research labs working in the same or similar area;
- participation in meetings of the academic team where the company can influence the direction of the research;
- the chance to directly or indirectly participate in the education of potential future employees and build awareness of access to specialists in a given area.

Case 4:
Atmosphere can enable openness

Keywords: Shared vision, learning together, system view, co-actualization.

Situation
In November 2012, the 4th Practice-Research Workshop, "Effective Communication in ICT Projects", took place in Vienna. The main aim of the workshop was to facilitate a sharing between representatives from the University of Vienna and Masaryk University Brno with numerous small and medium enterprises from Austria and the Czech Republic.

Participants had the opportunity to share their experiences in workshop groups. One of these workshop groups was titled "Openness and Dialog – How can the change from individual visions to a shared vision be achieved in a company?"

The workshop explored processes that lead to the development and explication of a shared vision, based on open statements of individual visions. The participants reflected upon the role of dialoguing in the context of team learning.

Scenario
During one of the workshop sessions, the participants created a mind map. First, they called the main node of the mind map "Openness/Dialogue". After some time, they changed the name to "Shared Vision". The facilitators collected statements of participants that were crystallization points of the group conversation.

During this session, everyone discussed the main obstacles preventing the transformation from individual visions to a shared vision. Participants revealed the following obstacles:
- Lack of support from management. Managers usually do not share the common vision of the company or the project with employees.
- Building "companies within companies". Departments do not share their own visions with each other.
- Complex hierarchy. Sharing vision is more complicated.
- Problems with achieving the shared vision. It usually introduces significant changes which can be uncomfortable for the team and hence tends not to be accepted by the team.
- Fixed habits of programmers. Developers may prefer the way they used to work to consequences of sharing a vision.

The rest of the session dealt with strategies for overcoming these obstacles. The emerging suggestions included:
- Increase communication and transparency in the team/company to give the team members a better chance to identify with the vision and the company.
- Don't teach programming and algorithms only. This produces students who have a very narrow view on the job of an IT specialist. They see the programming tasks as the only important thing, lose interest in anything else and become isolated in their world of statements. They become rigid and fixed.

Finally, one participant of the workshop stated as a reflection: "A good atmosphere in the working environment will lead to more inner confidence to contribute actively in the organization. It will fasten the identification with the company vision".

Comment

The vision of the project, a team or a whole company is the key element of a strategic planning. A vision sets out where we want the organization to go. And sharing the vision inspires and motivates all involved people – not only team members but also supporters (stakeholders, mentors and others).

A good vision helps everyone in the team to contribute. A vision is very valuable – especially in times of crisis when it helps to realize what is really important.

Invitation to reflect
- Do you think that a shared vision is really important?
- Did you establish such a vision for your project/company? Did your employees participate in creating the vision? Was it beneficial? Did employees report that it was a waste of time and if yes, what did you learn and how did you respond?
- Did you identify other obstacles or strategies for overcoming obstacles which you found also crucial when sharing a vision?

Insights
A shared vision is crucial in many aspects. When building a shared vision, the most important issue is to discuss it with the whole team. A vision created only by the top management will be hardly accepted by the rest of the team. Each member should have the opportunity to participate in forming the vision that gives him/her the feeling of being an important part of the chain.

As a result, this approach can attract and motivate the very best talents.

Potential strategies
The very basis of this problem reveals itself already in the IT education process. Developers should be trained not only in programming, but also in skills of communication and team collaboration. Then people are well prepared for sharing, influencing, and joining the shared vision of their future job.

> Ask yourself honestly:
> - How good is the atmosphere in your team/organization?
> - When did tension/uncertainties hinder innovation or change? Why?
> - How could you positively improve your environment?

Our insights

Christina:
Working in a motivated team where you feel save enough to express yourself openly, may for many people be more engaging and 'binding' then extrinsic incentives.

David:
People can grow in a rather threat-free environment, if circumstances are favorable for development.

Renate:
The atmosphere in teams is like the soil for plants. If it is good, growth and harvest are likely to be good too, even though there is no guarantee for this. If it is bad, maximum profit cannot be achieved for sure and the battle for survival becomes the primary concern.

Next steps to competencies

Which of the following ideas and suggestions make sense to you?

- Organization
  - You should be ensured that the vision of the organization is shared throughout the whole hierarchy of employees. Especially for newcomers, it is important to let them identify with the organization's vision and to determine where they could be most beneficial.

- Team
  - When your project requires cooperation, it is essential to care for the team and reward the skills and diligence of its members. But also keep in mind that it is possible to have too much "team". People like to get their work done and they like to leave work on time. So try to balance your demands and expectations with theirs.

- Individual
  - Each individual and his or her feelings strongly influence the atmosphere of other team members and even the whole organization. So if you are a team leader, always try to recognize changes in mood that can negatively affect the atmosphere. Do not ignore it. Though you will want to have patience, usually, the sooner you approach a problematic situation, the less impact the problem will have on team productivity. If you are an employee who is unsatisfied with some decision or situation, it may prove favorable not to hide or postpone it and discuss it with your boss. Maybe you will reveal that you are not the only person with the same opinion and consequentially the problem can be easily solved and both parts will be satisfied with it.

Final reflections

In what ways do you agree with these statements?

- The atmosphere in a team or organization contributes fundamentally to the quality of working life and to organizational and team performance and success. Since each individual contributes to the collective atmosphere, you cannot ignore anybody without damaging or at least scratching the atmosphere.
- Under proper conditions that are in part general and in part specific, flowers blossom. So do people.

Enable creativity in teams

To lead people, one needs to understand them, support their motivation and create the best possible environment that nurtures creativity for the best possible job performance.

Supporting motivation may not be easy – especially in highly creative environments. In this case you may need to approach team members as individuals and allow them to expand their competencies and grow within the company.

This means to create an atmosphere where your team will follow greater ideas, not just orders (see also the topic *"Care for the atmosphere"*). Allow team members to prosper and develop with the company so they feel like going somewhere, not just standing still.

Keywords: Management by competencies, creative team development, synergy, dynamic company, leadership.

Cases

Overview of cases

The cases tackle the issues of assembling a creative team, leadership, and working with talented people.

- Case 1 **"Building a creative team"** focuses on the way a team is created and how this influences its functionality, particularly when creativity is concerned. The case describes the preconditions which help to unleash creativity in a team from the beginning even under very difficult circumstances caused e.g. by budget limitations.

- Case 2 **"Formal versus "eye-level" leadership"** illustrates how an (in)appropriate approach to leading a team can either block or boost creativity. The case shows both a formal and an eye-level way to lead.

- Case 3 **"Managing a talented person"** shows how on the one hand, talented people are needed in every creative company; on the other hand, they might be difficult to approach and work with. The case presents first-hand experience from a start-up company.

Case 1:
Building a creative team

Keywords: Leadership, creativity, freedom, shared vision.

Situation
Creativity supports innovation within a company and allows business to grow. Moreover, new ideas and original solutions provide it with competitive advantages. Therefore, managers at all levels should always support creativity.

The presented case is based on a situation a rather small start-up company went through. The founder and CEO shared his experience in a discussion with an iCom team member.

Scenario
CEO: Chief Executive Officer   *Tom:* iCom team member

CEO: "We have started a company based on an idea of helping people and learning interesting things while transforming our vision to reality. We have managed to attract and keep about 10 people in the company without paying any salaries for over a year. We have not even promised any future company shares."

Tom: "How did you manage to engage – and retain – skilled people without paying them a single penny? Sounds like a miracle."

CEO: "The reasons that we can see behind such an achievement is supporting a common goal – a vision, a mission – and creating an environment which allows people to be creative and feel to be truly part of the company. Democratic discussions about what is happening in the company and setting current goals have been important parts of making everyone feel like a valuable member of the team. There have always been executives at the top but they were able to make decisions through leadership and gaining respect from others. But they also had to learn to trust the people in the company and accept the decision of the whole group at times."

Tom: "I see… Is sharing a vision and a mission a crucial part of motivation?"

CEO: "Creating a strong vision and a mission is very important. These should not become just empty definitions somewhere on the paper but company leaders should spread them by following them and communicating them directly *themselves*. Vision and mission are then able to provide a *framework for the team to which they relate their decisions and priorities* in development as well as in business. Preserving creativity and such an open environment in a small team is relatively easy but as the company grows it may become increasingly difficult and the leaders can start getting lost in company processes. A company's growth is always seen as a positive development but it has its pitfalls."

Tom: "So, you find the support of creativity, talents and making people live the company's vision to be a strong foundation leading to high efficiency and unexpected ideas and innovation?"

CEO: "Exactly."

Comment
Building a company culture that supports innovation and creativity is highly challenging and leaders often get lost in daily tasks instead of focusing on actively building an atmosphere in their company that supports personal growth of company members. Such an atmosphere is not about having a huge flat-screen TV and a game console in the common room but about creating and sharing values in the team.

> **Invitation to reflect**
> - What values does your company/organization have? How are those values communicated and who is or should be responsible for spreading them in your team?
> - Are your company values reflected in your products and/or services thus proving that the company is fulfilling its mission?
> - Is your company's vision/mission too general or does it give you a clear idea of its values?

Case 2:
Formal versus "eye level" leadership

Keywords: Delivery milestone, formal procedure, project team, social interaction, goodwill.

Situation
The project team is facing a delivery milestone. There are still some bugs in the software, and it is very likely that a high-quality delivery will require the team to work on Saturday, given the team is sufficiently motivated. The pressure and stress are quite high but everybody is giving it their best. However, there is a small setback – all the employees have flat-rate salaries and extra-hours are paid for only in exceptional situations. The given project does not allow for extra-payments due to its limited budget. As a consequence, the project manager depends on the good will of the team members to work on the upcoming Saturday.

The question is how would a project manager reveal to his or her team (Peter, Eva, Susan, and Felix) that he/she would like them to work on Saturday and give up the time off they deserve? Below, you will find two possible scenarios, a formal one and one that an industrial partner experienced, appreciated, and shared.

Scenario

Variant 1: Formal procedure
PM: Project Manager   **Peter, Susan, Felix, Eva:** Team members

PM: "I looked at the list of unresolved bugs. There are quite a few that we need to fix before delivery. And I spoke with the director. He said that we need to meet the deadline as the customer relies on it. This means that we'll need to work on the upcoming Saturday. Please take this into account. Unfortunately, there will be no extra money for that but I think that we all know how important it is to deliver on time."

Peter: "Why should I come? If the company does not care enough to pay me some extra for my hard work, why should I sacrifice my Saturday? And, by the way, I'm going to be done with my tasks by Friday!"

Susan: "Oh, great! I was given most of the tasks. Just because I've got more expertise in the field than the others I should come in on Saturday? I'm definitely not coming."

Felix and Eva pull a long face.
From this position it is practically impossible to motivate people to join in on extra work during the weekend.

Variant 2: Experienced eye-level procedure
PM: "During the last days we were quite successful with bug-fixing. It seems that we'll manage to meet Monday's delivery deadline. What is your estimate?"

Peter: "I'll be finished by Friday, no problem!"

Susan: "This is going to be really tight… and I don't think I'll manage to finish till Friday."

PM: "Mhm, can we help you with anything? Why not distribute the remaining tasks amongst the team. Felix and Eva, do you have some free resources?"

Felix: "Absolutely not. I'm not going to be able to finish till Friday, Peter already gave me two bugs because I can fix them more quickly."

Eva: "I need to tend to the quality assurance – so even if the others finish on Friday I certainly won't."

PM: Pause, looks to the ground. "I can't postpone Monday's milestone. Furthermore, we would really benefit from making the delivery on time so that we can deal with the next steps in relative peace. I realize that we're currently working to the limit, but the sooner this is over the better. What do you think?"

Eva: "You're certainly right. I can't even look at the test cases any more…"

PM (Smiling): "Yeah. I don't like it either. And the same goes for quality assurance. (to Eva) I'm going to help you with it. I'd be willing to come here on Saturday, would it be an option for you then to come in?"

Eva: "Definitely not an option that I would enjoy."

PM: "That makes two of us. So at least you won't be alone. Are there any other volunteers who'd be willing to sacrifice their Saturday? You'd get my undying appreciation and immortal fame, plus I'd supply you with pizza."

Peter: "If you find a bug in my module, I'll come and fix it. I hope you can afford the loads of salami that we're gonna need on our pizzas!"

Comment

The project team in variant 2 managed to deliver a high quality milestone. In the end, the Saturday was quite short and enjoyable.

> **Invitation to reflect**
> - What made the project manager in variant 2 succeed?
> - Do you think that the eye-level situation as described above could be somehow learned? If yes, try to explain how, if not, give some reasons why you think it cannot be learned.

Insights

If you get truly involved in the problem you can become a part of the solution. The eye-level situation as described above is not a recipe that would always work. It needs to arise from the situation and the relationships involved.

Potential strategies
In case of success or failure, take some time to reflect on what went well and what did not, how you feel about it, and what you might want to do differently the next time.

Case 3:
Managing a talented person

Keywords: Leadership, teams, talent management.

Situation
The CEO of a start-up company considers: "Every innovative company needs highly talented people as driving forces of its activities. Some talented people are so overly sure of their skills and intelligence that they feel they are never wrong and everyone who disagrees with their opinion is making a big mistake. Such attitudes indicate poor social skills and make teamwork rather difficult. Especially in cases when two people are being absolutely sure about their different truths, the situation can escalate."

Scenario
The case is based on the experience of participants in a small start-up.

CEO: Chief Executive Officer   *Tom:* iCom team member

The *CEO* reports: "In our company we had a highly talented graphic designer responsible for user experience design. He always felt strongly about his opinions and was often right even when others would not agree with him at first. There is nothing that could be said against his skills. However, most people found it difficult to work with him in a team because his skills always came with a sort of inherited arrogance. The issue became more serious when the task was discussed with similarly talented and strong-minded people."

Tom: "Have you tried to convince him that he is not always right?"

CEO: "The trouble is that these people *usually are right*. They are professionals who dominate their field of expertise. When managing such people, communication is absolutely crucial. The manager needs to be aware of the situation and actively listen to receive feedback from the other people around. The talented person needs to feel that he/she is being listened to and that the manager understands what he/she is saying."

Tom: "So what was it that did the trick this time?"

CEO: "He always needed the faults in his behavior and communication to be explained rationally. For him, explaining his opinion to the other team members was sort of *a waste of his valuable time*. Primarily, we had to convince him to understand that if he sacrifices a few minutes of his time it makes the other people more *motivated and effective* and they will appreciate *his effort* more. That *him taking this small step means a huge leap for the team*."

Tom: "So you actually accepted his, if I may say, selfish nature?"

CEO [laughing]: "Indeed. We managed to turn his communication 'difficulties' into an advantage. Yes, it took me more time. Talented people usually need more attention from their manager. It is not possible to change their nature or mentality; however, one can teach them to understand teamwork and its rules. They need to feel that teamwork *empowers rather* than limits them, and they can benefit from it."

Insights

The CEO of the start-up company concludes: "*Communication* appears to be of utmost importance here. You can hardly change someone's nature or temperament but as a manager/leader, you should be respected and able to moderate difficult situations.

If you succeed you will be rewarded with your team's high efficiency and increased potential. Respect talented people and do not treat them as a boss. Their intelligence probably comes with an ego that has hard time accepting orders from anyone. It is better to be able to explain to them why they should be doing their tasks and why those tasks are important and should be done in a certain way."

Invitation to reflect
- Do you know some highly intelligent people around you who are difficult to work with? How did you handle the *last encounter* with them?
- Do you perhaps consider yourself to be such a person, maybe just in some situations/roles?

Our insights

Inappropriate ways of communication with creative and talented people may easily lead to a disaster. An innovative organization cannot survive without fully involving its team members. Leadership, sharing a vision, active listening, patience, humility, and rational arguments may help to achieve a productive balance between individuality and common goals.

Next steps to competencies

Do the following ideas make sense to you?

- Organization
  - Sharing a common vision within the team prevents frustration and boosts the productivity of the creative process. An open discussion, rational arguments and feeling of acceptance can help.

- Team
  - An inclusive atmosphere and feeling of togetherness among the highly-talented team members should be achieved consciously by actively listening to and respecting each other.

- Individual
  - We may accept diversity of personalities in a team/organization and see it rather as an enriching factor than an obstacle.

References

Cornelius-White, J. H. D., Motschnig, R., & Lux, M. (2013). *Interdisciplinary Applications of the Person-Centered Approach.* New York: Springer Science & Business.

Constructive Communication

Communication matters, cultivate it

Good communication is a key enabler for collaboration and relationships. **In the professional world, it is not just a way to transfer information between communicating parties, it is about setting up an environment for collaboration by establishing a *Shared vision* and further elaborating it by *Co-actualization.*** Non-functioning communication can be attributed to many different causes:

- Mistrust leads to hiding (see topic: *"Hiding consumes energy"*) and disrupts productive communication.
- Lack of time is certainly one enemy of communication, as *active listening* cannot be applied. The motivations and reasons of both parties as well as their feelings cannot be fully uncovered.
- A lack of (geographical) proximity can be a barrier, but using appropriate online communication tools for talking, messaging, and conferencing can improve the situation. Anyway, *Face-to-face* meetings are still crucial to apply active listening, recognize the feelings, and ensure common understanding at a personal level enabling co-actualization.
- However, the distance caused by different positions in a hierarchy complicates, distorts or even prevents productive communication, and can be overcome by trust and meeting at eye level (see topic: *"Meeting at eye level opens doors"*).

The potential stumbling blocks for constructive communication increase when communicating in an international environment, in part because language-related problems are added to the mix. The ability to express oneself in a foreign language is usually weaker and requires more effort than in the mother tongue. It may lead to unintentional hiding of information or nuances crucial to understand the position and feelings of the communicating party. In a non-symmetric situation when one communicates in his/her mother language and the other one does not, the other one might feel handicapped or it can be discouraging for being open. However, choosing a "neutral" language, which is non-native for both parties, does not prevent all problems. Rather, it can block both parties from fully and openly expressing their feelings as both cannot find the right words. So, if struggling to find the essence of an issue, using the native language might be more helpful, even when it leads to partial separation of communication into "native language groups" before re-joining the communication.

People in leading positions tend to ask questions such as:
- How can I improve my communication skills to be a more effective leader or manager?
- What is it that I want to improve in my communication? How can I do this most effectively?

Keywords: Co-actualization, international communication, knowledge sharing, conflict resolution, academic-industrial cooperation, shared vision, decision-making, strategic decision, hiding of information, learning from cases, sensing, multiple perspectives, transparency, learning together, shared vision, meeting at eye level, getting closer, similarity and difference, complex understanding, flow of information (transparency), dialogue.

Cases

Overview of cases

- Case 1 **"The language of the workshop is English, right?"** examines that deciding on a common language is not trivial, as the language spoken has effects on the group.

- Case 2 **"Dialogue takes time"** elicits that the right time planning and management allows creativity.

- Case 3 **"Really internationalized environment?"** portrays that internationalization cannot be enforced by rules only, but must be lived.

- Case 4 **"No shared vision kills cooperation before it starts"** highlights that communicating a shared vision is particularly important for partners with different primary goals.

Case 1:
The language of the workshop is English, right?

Keywords: Workshop language, language understanding, English, translation, inclusion, exclusion, cross-cultural team authenticity.

Situation
All understand English and speak it sufficiently well to make oneself understood – so the workshop language will be English, no doubt! Isn't this the only way that makes sense in an international workshop?

Scenario
In the iCom experience we were confirmed that English can be used as a language that reaches all workshop participants more or less. The basic content was transported to all partners and many of them participated in the interactive parts, some speaking more, others less, as always. We were all in "the same boat", English not being our native language. But it served its purpose – to make oneself understood on a basic level. Often, a helpful colleague could supply a missing word, and conversation flowed.

Nevertheless, as soon as a break started, participants often formed small groups with their linguistic mates, immediately staring to use their language, making jokes, telling stories and laughing together. The heaviness of having to express oneself in a less familiar language vanished, energy came back, and a lot more words flew between partners than when they were expressing themselves in English. Even when sitting at the lunch table, local conversations were often in the partners' native tongue, the one that could be managed with most ease.

A keynote speaker who expressed his or her welcome sentence in the local language(s) immediately tended to have the audience's hearts on his side and make them smile about the fun accent he had. It seems that using one's native language, be it only to express a greeting or a word can be an icebreaker, and it radiates respect to the other if this is what is also felt internally.

The author of this case, a true fan of English, came to the international projects with little doubt that English is the language to use in workshops since all knew it to some degree. Anything else would unnecessarily complicate the world. While staying a fan of English, I'm leaving the "Constructive international communication in the context of ICT" project with a more differentiated sensing of people's "natural" needs to be more authentic and to use their languages whenever appropriate. But what is appropriate in this context?

As a reader you may want to formulate your own response. In case you're interested on what the author's colleagues think, read on:

View of a team leader: "The reason why this particular workshop was largely held in German was due to *business partners* from the Vienna (i.e. German-speaking) region. It started intentionally in English but continued spontaneously in German. The German-speaking business partners felt comfortable and included in the project, which was fine for its smooth takeoff. As some of the participants from the Czech Republic were also *personally* comfortable with this setting, it took a lot of time before a problem of exclusion of the non-German speaking participants was detected and recognized. So, my main experience gained is that *when we want to support inclusion, we should prevent simultaneous exclusion.*"

View of a project manager: "I believe that the language issue depends on the context. From my experience, communicating in your native language makes it easier to express yourself without being misunderstood. For very personal or sensitive issues, one's mother tongue is preferable as in translating some things might get lost.

On the other hand, when working with international people I feel that using a language everybody understands is a sign of respect. When we intend to unite people in cross-border projects or activities, I think it is essential to use a common language – both in formal settings as well as informal conversations."

View of another team leader: "To me, it seems that a key issue is not to exclude others by speaking more than very few words in a language they can't follow. This holds true for presentations as well as for talks at the lunch table."

Invitation to reflect
- What language do you use when meeting persons from your country at international conferences?
- How do you feel if people use their language that you don't understand?
- How do you feel about using English whenever possible?

Insights
The issue of language is not a simple one – language is deeply ingrained. Usually, common sense, respect and good will to facilitate as much understanding as possible will lead to creative solutions. These, however, will tend to vary from situation to situation.

Potential strategies
To ensure better understanding, very brief previews or summaries in local languages could be foreseen to complement a presentation held in English, given a simultaneous translation can't be accommodated or is not considered necessary.

Too strict "artificial rules" seem to be counterproductive. Felt respect toward the other person and a desire to understand and be understood tend to be desirable values for facilitating a climate that is conductive to the forming of contacts.

In the long-term run, improving language skills, learning each other's language is the best way to feel comfortable independent of the language.

Case 2:
Dialogue takes time

Keywords: Group discussion, atmosphere, personal insights.

Situation
In the group on team learning, people started to share their personal insights just at the end of a 1.5-hour workshop. It is likely that more time would have enabled deeper sharing and unlocked creativity and productivity. However, the time limit was known in advance, so managing the group dynamics could have also helped the dialogue takeoff faster.

Scenario

A similar scenario repeats many times during the iCom cross-border project: A session on a certain topic is organized, either a PhD-course or a workshop, with attendance of the interested public. The participants from both collaborating teams usually meet in the morning. As they have not seen each other for at least a couple of weeks, a series of individual discussions begins. If it is an open event such as a workshop, there are new participants who influence the atmosphere and bring moments of curiosity to the team members. In some situations, somebody new (either formally or informally) leads the session. Frequently, his/her approach and new unexpected ideas make the discussion slower at the beginning and distract from reaching the planned goals quickly and straightforwardly. Some group members do not feel comfortable with this situation as they expect fast progress towards attaining the foreseen target. It takes a while before the whole group gets to the same conceptual level and is able to concentrate on the matter. Eventually, it usually happens, but sometimes the scheduled time is just about over.

> **Invitation to reflect**
> - Do you have experiences with such situations? If yes, how frequently does it happen in your workshops, meetings, and sessions?
> - Do you consciously introduce specific measures to eliminate it, such as a kind of "warm-up" exercise at the beginning of a session? Or do you use strict time scheduling in all cases and prevent it?

Insights

In loosely coupled teams and communities it is difficult to eliminate, but in established teams it should not occur regularly.

It takes some time before real dialogue begins. If we want to achieve it, we must ensure enough time. Appropriate setting (environment, moderation, and time management) is inevitable for achieving a particular type of results.

Group dynamics play an important role in establishing an atmosphere of trust and openness needed for learning and creative work.

Case 3:
Really internationalized environment?

Keywords: International environment, different management styles, closed vs. open environment, communication in foreign language, meeting at eye level.

Situation
There were a series of misunderstandings related to a visit of a foreign expert and a clash between two management styles under stressful conditions in an international environment and foreign language communication. The situation involved a lack of communication and not meeting at eye level.

Scenario
A visiting expert came to an academic institution for a 3-month visit. He wanted to share as much as possible from his experience. Together with the responsible person from the hosting institution, a series of scientific and educational activities was planned and agreed before the visit. The activities included a block-course. The course was offered for all relevant students who did not yet participate in a similar course taught by local experts. Neither financial compensation nor any additional effort was required from the organizers of the original local course. So, the visiting expert and the leader of the hosting lab had the impression that the block-course given by the visiting expert would *be welcome by the local experts* as an authentic international contribution for the students. The visiting expert and the leader of the hosting lab continued to prepare further steps to make the course reality.

The first problems appeared shortly after the block-course was officially announced. The local experts reacted quickly and negatively, claiming that the block-course would *distract the students from taking the original local one*. After making the visiting expert's course formally an alternative to the original one, the initial resistance was suppressed and the situation calmed. It ended up with a setup of two groups – one from the original local course given by local experts and the second one natively international by the visiting expert.

However, the idea of the visiting expert was not to make "just another instance" of the original local course but to put in *his best effort to shift the course to a higher, truly international level*. Moreover, the two groups could participate together in a common final output to see the advantages of each approach – the original and the new one. So, there emerged a couple of ideas to enrich the course as a whole – both the original group and the new one, and to do as much as possible together in order to take the best from both approaches to enhance the course in a sustainable way.

A short *face-to-face meeting* was organized to discuss the proposals of the visiting expert with the local organizers. The meeting was extremely brief and actually did not take the form of a discussion but information flowed in one direction from the local organizers on "how the common final session should look". The local organizers did not *actively listen* to the visiting expert. It was certainly not a *meeting at eye level*.

All together, the local resistance led to denial of almost all proposals for improvement:
- The idea of having a separate competition category for posters elaborated as outcomes from the course under the guidance of the visiting expert has been refused by local organizers as unfair and discriminating, not providing equal opportunities to all participants.
- The proposal to include a "PechaKucha" session with flash presentations of the posters before the actual competition was also denied.
- An improved version of the "book of proceedings" from the final poster session with more detailed descriptions, better graphics, and higher-quality printing was finally done just for the visiting expert's group and not for the other one.
- The final poster competition was entirely carried out the very same way as ever before, including the use of the local language instead of English though the students are strongly encouraged to write the posters in English. The local experts did not take the visiting expert as a "special guest judge" in the competition but rather did the poster evaluation in the local language leaving the visiting expert excluded from the process.

The effort of the visiting expert to enrich the poster preparation course was to large extent undermined by local resistance trying to keep the things going as ever before. The meeting, which should serve as a discussion platform to find a common solution, was much more a briefing than a discussion.

Probably, the local organizers entirely underestimated the seriousness of the situation, which included foreign guests coming to do their best for the hosting institution. They actually forgot to think in the interest of the students as the target group of the poster preparation block-course.

> **Invitation to reflect**
> - What, in your opinion, was the fatal flaw?
> - If you could act as "deus ex machina" and intercept the process from outside, what would you do and when?
> - As the leader of the hosting lab was the only person involved in all processes, including those that are entirely local and not transparent for the outside world, what would you recommend to him?
> - Is there anything that can be recommended to prevent similar uncomfortable situations in the future?

Insights

Providing a service for a particular target group – and educational or developmental activities are always services for the others – requires sensitivity and goal orientation. Our position within the problem should always be less important than the goal to be achieved.

Listen to anybody who wants to help us, regardless if it changes our way of doing things.

Case 4:
No shared vision kills the cooperation before it starts

Keywords: Shared vision, hidden agenda, academic-industrial collaboration.

Situation

Many times the companies from the ICT-industry enthusiastically, even eagerly, grasp for the chance to have an academic partner (Faculty of Informatics, Masaryk University in our case). However, it frequently – in around half of the cases – gets stuck after they reach the first goal, which is recruitment, without further strong commitment to do real collaboration. The causes typically include a missing shared, commonly agreed, vision at all relevant levels. Missing effort to elaborate the vision.

Scenario

The Faculty of Informatics at Masaryk University has a tradition in institutionalized industrial cooperation taking the form of participation in its *Association of Industrial Partners*. The Association works on basis of bilateral university-company agreements declaring common interests and setting up general goals of the future bilateral cooperation.

The Faculty was always trying to lower the entrance barriers for joining the Association. The companies, potential partners of the Faculty, are offered a wide spectrum of activities they can participate in and profit from. The activities are in general of two distinct kinds: human-resources-oriented, aimed at attracting students (graduates) as competent, well-educated, highly skilled staff into the company. The second kind involves a set of more problem-oriented activities focused on joint research and development, starting from joint supervision of students' graduation projects, but including also larger research projects in cooperation.

Quite frequently, we face the following scenario during the further cooperation. If the company is innovative and experienced in academic-industrial cooperation, it knows the pros and cons of academic cooperation and explicitly tries to identify common areas of interests in research and development (R&D). Then a lab/team as well as a responsible contact person is found at the Faculty. If the company has no previous experience, it simple does not know what to expect and let the process run its own way. The company visits twice a year the regular meetings of the Association, which include separate sessions for students and a meeting with Faculty's top management.

The company thus achieves at least partial satisfaction with hiring current students and future graduates by the company. Many companies stop at this moment being saturated in their needs. For many of them, however, this is a unique undertaking and they even leave the Association having no further interests on continuation.

It is then, on the other hand, *frustrating for the responsible contact person* once he/she invested time and effort to find the right content of the collaboration. In some cases the contact person is not active enough to find the area of cooperation and the partnership dissolves before it really begins.

Invitation to reflect
- Do you think the mistakes in communication between the Faculty and the future industrial partner are more *individual* (depending on concrete case and people involved) or do they have a more *systematic nature*?
- Where is, in your opinion, the substantial "breakpoint" in the communication, after which the things go (inevitably) wrong?

Insights

In most cases, there is good will from both sides. However, it can still lead to dissatisfaction and interruption of the cooperation due to many reasons, particularly *not engaging the right people* at the right time to initiate and continue the cooperation. Human resource (HR) experts might not be the optimal leaders of manifold cooperations including joint R&D as their primary goal is quite narrow – find and draft the HR for the company. However, the same applies to researchers that were nominated as the responsible contact persons from the Faculty. Experienced in their fields, focused at their R&D, but easily overlooking the *real* goals of the industrial partners, particularly the HR-oriented ones, which are usually out of their normal scope.

Finding the right responsible person to conduct the discussions about a shared long-term vision is an enormously difficult task. The crucial question is whether the primary professional role of the person includes establishing the shared vision. Or do they just partially overlap? The latter position is not sufficient to establish a shared vision.

A *systematic approach* had to be taken in order to prevent further dissatisfaction. The management of the Association of Industrial Partners (stakeholders form the Faculty) decided to specify the *conditions for partnership in more details in the agreement*. So, a kind of "predefined" or "default" shared vision has been proposed to each partner. It led to confusion of some partners, even those where the problems had not emerged yet. In some cases, it took much more time to sign the agreement.

Our insights

The cases illustrating this topic tackle some important aspects of cross-border and cross-cultural communication. Primarily, communication always needs a common language, but choosing a common language is not always the best option and should not be applied blindly. Secondly, any communication takes time before it leads to a conclusion and brings results; so careful scheduling and sensitive moderation of communication-intensive events is a must. Thirdly, choosing the right language is just one aspect of really functional international cooperation. Acceptance and mutual respect of all the parties is at least equally important. Finally, there is no fruitful collaboration if there is no shared vision, which is to be achieved through communicating it.

Next steps to competencies

Do the following ideas make sense to you?

- Organization
  - Some rules to encourage certain communication styles within a team or organization are necessary. This holds particularly for internationally (culturally) mixed ones.

- Team
  - The team is the best place to learn communication skills, if it provides a save learning environment. Active listening may be the right starting point.

- Individual
  - Do not feel offended. Mostly, it is not about you, it is about a problem at work.

Final reflections

In what ways do you agree with the subsequent statement?
- Very general principles like being *open* and *listen actively* look trivial but are not just meaningless words. If taken seriously, they help to improve the organizational climate.

References

Cornelius-White, J.H.D., Motschnig, R., & Lux, M. (Eds.) (2013). *Interdisciplinary Applications of the Person-Centered Approach.* New York: Springer Science & Business.

Rogers, C. R., & Farson, R. E. (1987). *Active listening.* Excerpt from Communicating in Business Today. [Available online http://www.go-get.org/pdf/Rogers_Farson.pdf]

Senge, P. (2006). *The Fifth Discipline, The Art & Practice of the Learning Organization.* New York: Currency Doubleday.

Further resources:
Here is a reference to a study examining the impact of Person-centered Communication (PCC) on leader-member relationship and job satisfaction. The results indicated significant positive relationships between PCC and leader-member relationship, as well as between PCC and employee job satisfaction.

Fix, B., & Sias, P. M. (2006). Person-Centered Communication, Leader-Member Exchange, and Employee Job Satisfaction. *Journal Communication Research Reports, 23*(1), 35-44.

Meeting at eye level opens doors

Meeting another person as a person rather than interacting with him or her as a position or role is a privilege, indeed. When you can literally look each other straight into the eyes, you can share whatever you consider appropriate. There is no formal matter that per se interferes with your encountering the other. The quality of meeting each other at eye level tends to have a special connecting flow usually not present in hierarchic relationships (see also topic *"Transparency yields flow"*).

To capture more concretely what meeting at eye level means and what it does not mean let us consider a few examples. Meeting at eye level is not to hide behind some professional role; it is not to play the expert, to patronize, to blame the other or to distance oneself from responsibilities. It is to be present for the other as well as oneself, to try to understand the other, to listen, be vulnerable and to risk to be changed when encountering the other person. In other words, when meeting others at eye level both parties are in a continual learning mode, looking out for solutions to complex problems together, often in a creative, non-standard way. Meeting someone at eye level also means to understand and accept a person as a unique individual. Some general assumptions might be applicable, others not. This becomes especially relevant in intercultural encounters in which many of our learned constructs may not apply. Cultural awareness, respect for otherness and empathy are extremely helpful for building good relationships and enhancing the quality of co-working.

In the context of a project team, team members and users can profit from meeting at eye level. Bringing together different areas of expertise may be challenging at first, but the project team may get a lot out of increased knowledge on various levels, better relationships to the customers, a feeling of belonging in the group. Holding different job positions, e.g. team leader and team member, does not necessarily exclude meeting the other at eye level, though in the beginning, meeting eye-to-eye is better to come from the person holding the higher position. So why not sit down for lunch with your team? Why not be in close contact? The more you know about your team and the more contact you have with them, the more informal (important!) information and insights will be shared. Additionally, you will reduce the barrier employees often face in approaching their team leader with any problems, questions and bright ideas (see topic *"Every perspective is valuable"*).

So, what tends to promote meeting at eye level?

What can you do in a particular situation or relationship to get into eye-level contact?

What are the benefits of eye-level contact and are there pitfalls and situations where you better avoid meeting person-to-person?

Keywords: Interpersonal relationship, relationship person-to-person, eye-level, interdependence, listening, positive regard, openness, trust, authenticity, transparency, reflection.

Cases

Overview of cases

The cases of this topic take different approaches to illustrate what can happen – and how the world looks different – if people manage to meet person-to-person.

- Case 1 **"Incomplete requirements: Different ways of meeting your employee"** takes up the ever recurring theme of "incomplete requirements". It illustrates different ways in which managers can meet their team members in the context of this often complicated challenge.

- Case 2 **"Authoritarian versus understanding teacher"** uses dialogue excerpts to juxtapose the conversation between a pupil and an "authoritative versus understanding teacher". Drawing parallels to work contexts and turning challenging behavior into support are inspired in the reflection part of the case.

- Case 3 **"Dynamics of strategic decisions"** brings us back to the work context and intends to let readers muse about the often strange "dynamics of strategic decisions" such as to be prepared if already decided issues get questioned in a new light.

- Finally, Case 4 **"Reflection and sharing of experience with your employees"** intends to draw the reader's attention to the issue of "reflection and sharing of experience with your employees" as a means of life-long learning for all involved.

Case 1:
Incomplete requirements: Different ways of meeting your employee

Keywords: Requirements specification, incomplete requirements, blaming, self-organization, trust, motivation.

Situation
The following two conversations reflect two different approaches to the problem of incomplete requirements. How do they resonate with you? How would you describe/label each of them?

Scenario

Variant 1:
M: Manager   *TM:* Team Member

M: (with a probing voice) "Did you deliver the system at client McDuck?"

TM: "Not quite. They brought some old data sets that our database didn't upload."

M: "How could this happen?"

TM: (defensively) "It was not specified precisely. Who could have known that they wanted to import from ancient Oracle versions!"

M: (upset) "Why was this not included in the specification? You know that omissions and errors in the specification can be very costly!"

TM: (explaining) "We had specified data imports from Oracle databases and tested their samples from back to version 5. The representative from McDuck gave still older data to be uploaded, and they hold the position that these datasets must be handled."

M: "So either you can deliver this extension within the next three days or we need to argue that these very old versions are not part of the contract! Why the hell is there always something not working properly!?!"

TM: (submissively) "I'll work on it as soon as possible. Clients can be nasty, indeed."

Variant 2:
M: (with an interested voice) "Did you deliver the system at client McDuck?"

TM: "Not quite. They brought some old data sets that our database didn't upload."

M: "I see. (pause) They brought some old formats that they wanted to have uploaded, hmm, and I assume this was not explicitly specified beforehand? (looks up to TM, TM nods his head for approval) (pause, then with a voice expressing curiosity and openness) Well, what is your sense of this situation?"

TM: (thoughtfully, kind of thinking aloud) "Well, as far as I know, they need those datasets for statistical purposes, so I'd indeed like to extend the code to cover this. (pause) I guess I need to take a look at how much effort this means. I assume it's not a big issue and I can resolve this soon or ask them for extension. (genuinely, after a short pause) My sense indeed is that the way we deal with each other this time will be decisive for any future contacts!"

M: (frankly) "Makes sense to me. Just go ahead and let me know whenever you need me. Good luck, great to have you 'on board'!"

Comment
While the team member in variant 1 is receiving orders and works just to satisfy a "nasty customer", the team member in variant 2 is working from his or her own conviction and is truly motivated to make a positive difference in the customer's and the manager's experience.

Invitation to reflect
- How would you label variant 1 and variant 2, respectively?
- Do you think that the manager's attitude toward the team member will have an influence on how the team deals with customers?
- How do you estimate the level of motivation to resolve the case in each of the situations?
- How does the manager establish or avoid meeting the team member at eye level? How does the team member react?
- What would be your way of dealing with a situation similar to that encountered in the scenarios? Would you have some general "strategy" or would it totally depend on the other person and the customer?
- Can you recall experiences at your workplace that either variant 1 or variant 2 evoked in you? In settings similar to situation 1, (how) could *you* have contributed to a solution more oriented towards situation 2?

Insights
Attitudes are contagious. As the manager, you have an enormous influence to contribute to forming the interpersonal climate not only of your team but also of your and their relationships with the customer.

Potential strategies
Why not start a conversation with the basic anticipation that the other person can be trusted – unless proven the opposite? A default positive anticipation is more likely to bring out a positive, constructive reaction than an assumption of incompetence or bad intention. This does not mean to blindly trust endlessly, it only means an initialization towards a positive end. The process itself will bring evidence on how it unfolds and call for adjustment, but a positive initial kickoff tends to cost little and import positive energy.

Case 2:
Authoritarian versus understanding teacher

Keywords: Teacher-pupil interaction, authoritarian teacher, listening for understanding, computer games, empowerment.

This case originates in a school context and illustrates the "pure culture" of the issue at hand. It is intended, though, to be understood in any context in which one person is in charge of others.

Situation
Depending on the teacher's personality and attitudes, one and the same situation – in this case a pupil playing computer games in class – can be handled in different ways, leaving different traces on the learner's experience and motivation.

Scenario
Variant 1: An authoritarian teacher finds a pupil playing computer games in his lesson.

T: Teacher   *P:* Pupil

T: "Hey, I see you're playing these damn computer games in my lessons."

P: "I'm sorry but I'm so bored."

T: "Aha, you say you're bored. I can help you out with some extra exercises. Look at your classmates. Are they bored? I have more than 10 years of school experience and all pupils so far have found excitement in my lessons and exercises. No pupil ever got bored!"

P: "I'm not bored by your exercises but …"

T: "Come on, stop inventing excuses. If you are such a bright pupil, you're very welcome to do an extra exercise. This I do only for you, you super talent!"

P: (whispering to himself) "Teachers are so unfair. …. I hate school. Wish I could be sick and stay at home next lesson."

Variant 2: A teacher with a high degree of person-centered attitudes finds a pupil playing computer games in his lesson

T: "Hi, how are you today?"

P: "Thanks, quite well. I finished my assignments and will occupy myself with playing some computer games."

T: "So the computer game serves you as a kind of gap-filling activity to bridge the time to the next break?"

P: "Yes. You know, I don't really like the game – but what else should I do?"

T: "If I hear you correctly, you don't like the game but don't know how you could spend the time?"

P: "Exactly, computer science can become so boring."

T: "In computer science you rather want to engage in exciting activities that challenge you."

P: "Maybe, but I don't want to do an extra exercise."

T: "You want to do the same assignments as your peers but you're done fast and then boredom comes upon you. Can you imagine that somehow your peers could benefit from your experience?"

P: "Maybe, I haven't asked them. I guess they think I'm a freak or so."

T: "This frightens you a bit, you don't want to be considered a freak."

P: "Yeah. I don't know what they'd think if I offered them my support. But sure I think I could help them since I see that some of them are lost in particular situations."

T: "So you could help me to explain some issues to your classmates."

S: "Ok. You could introduce me as your assistant in some tasks, and I could help."

T: "Perfect, I'll do that and I'm convinced we all will profit from our collaboration!"

S: "I'm nervous but excited about that and looking forward to the next lesson."

Comment

While in variant 1, one person dominates the other and uses his position to exert power, in variant 2, both persons meet the other with respect. This reciprocity of positively valuing the other instead of blaming is evident from the first interchange onward and tends to grow during the conversation.

> **Invitation to reflect**
> - What is different in approaching the problem in the 2nd variant?
> - Do you know similar situations in your work context?
> - What effects did your teachers have on your current or previous occupation?
> - Which teachers motivated you and how could they achieve this?

Insights

After listening to the other's needs and wants, collaborative solutions that benefit both parties are likely to be found, as illustrated in variant 2.

Assumptions about the other without any listening to him or her and thus without grounding have a high probability of being largely false.

Potential strategies

Try to meet the other person where he/she is, and if you are not sure, ask. Assuming bad intentions upfront can put one on the defensive – but what sense does this make if there is no real or intended attack?

Sometimes understanding the intention behind some behavior can provide valuable information. It could be used for developing a win-win solution instead of attacking each other.

Case 3:
Dynamics of strategic decisions

Keywords: Meeting at eye level, pro-active behavior, shared vision, strategic thinking, decision-making.

Situation
A strategically important project connected to establishing a Science Park at a major university has been prepared under time pressure. The core decision to submit the proposal was taken at the beginning by consensus, then confirmed at another strategic forum and later disputed as "not sufficiently discussed".

Scenario
Structurally, there are two decision-making bodies A and B which are responsible for the Science Park. A strategically important project connected to the Science Park has been prepared under time pressure by a member of the body B. The core decision to submit the proposal was taken at the beginning by consensus at a face-to-face meeting of A with the author of the proposal. Later, when almost completed, it was confirmed at B. The final decision was to be done by A, which later disputed the proposal as "not sufficiently discussed".

There were several notable circumstances:

The project was understood as having strategic meaning by B but not really by A. A, however, being the ultimate decision maker and project hosting, felt more responsible in terms of sustainability and the financial aspects than B. Subsequently, A generally underestimated the role of B.

During the process taking approximately two months, there was neither face-to-face nor online communication between A and B, though they were not isolated and had personal intersections. Particularly, there was no meeting at eye level between representatives of A and B at all. As a consequence, there was probably no shared notion what had actually been agreed in each phase of the process. Finally, after A introduced quite serious changes to the proposal, an approval for the proposal was given.

Invitation to reflect
- What communication methods could help to avoid such a situation?
- Would you recommend any changes in the decision processes/structures to prevent problems like this?
- What is your impression of team A? Can you imagine why they acted as described?
- Have you observed any consequences that happen to complex strategic plans if they are put to rest for some time?
- Based on your insight and experience, what would you do if you were a member of B to whom the proposal was important?

Insights

The primary source of disputes throughout the whole process is the lack of a precise understanding of what exactly was accepted by consensus at the initial meeting of A and what implications this would have for the parties involved. What actually did each party expect as next steps? A shared notion of what has really been agreed in each step is vital.

Important decisions take time.

It is always good to openly and explicitly emphasize the strategic meaning of some activity or decision because it is often not automatically understood by all decision-makers though they are expected to be aware of it.

Pro-active behavior of all participants including open communication in such situations prevents later misunderstandings. Ask to clarify potential disputes before it is too late.

Even under stressful circumstances (e.g., time pressure, potential serious consequences of a decision), concentration "on the ball" rather than "on the player" helps to stay focused to the real problem and be constructive. It strengthens the common feeling and releases some of the stress.

Case 4:
Reflection and sharing of experience with your employees

Keywords: Self-assessment, feedback, evaluation.

Situation
Meeting at eye level also means to grant employees the autonomy to evaluate themselves rather than (or in addition to) evaluating them from an external perspective. Granting that freedom and furthermore demonstrating interest by listening to what the other shares communicates respect to the other person as an interdependent individual rather than seeing him or her as an object of evaluation and measurement. Similarly, asking the other for feedback tends to bring him/her in, making them think and potentially integrating their perspective. This can feel very motivating, indeed.

Scenario
During a yearly appraisal meeting between manager and employee:
M: Manager   *T:* Team Member

M: "How satisfied are you with the project so far and how do you see your particular contribution?"

T: "Well, we're pretty well pursuing the project plan and delivering the milestones. Formally everything is in place in my view. I organized the last two workshops and the participants' feedback and attendance is positive. Personally, however, I wish the project could have more impact with all the work we're investing into it. Helping companies integrate our ideas is a tedious process and I wish I could accelerate it but don't know how."

M: "I see and get exactly the same impression. We could have more impact. Recently I thought we should send some material to the press and have them write an article. What do you think?"

T: "This is certainly a good idea. We could send them for example X and invite them to participate in a round table on "initiating interregional collaborations" during the next workshop. This would improve the dissemination, and we would become better known in the public."

M: "I like your suggestion with the round table – let's plan this for the next event. In the meantime we assemble a selection of material including X and send them to our press contact list. But I think you had something else on your mind when mentioning your – could I say – frustration with the slow penetration of our ideas into company's lives?"

T: "Yes, it comes close to "frustration", maybe it's more my "impatience" with actual changes that do happen but much too slowly and in a rather shallow way only."

M: (Nods his head) "I think I know what you mean. So is there something I/we can do to support you and the project in this respect?"

T: "I'm not sure. Maybe we'd need more intensive and frequent contact with the business partners. But where could we take the necessary time resources? Everybody is so busy all the time. …"

Comment
Reflection tends to call for meeting oneself at eye level. If this can be communicated to the other person and is taken into account, it has the potential to establish a setting of regard and trust towards the other person. He/she is not (only) evaluated from an external authority but can be the authority him- or herself. Similarly, asking another person for how they experienced a situation communicates interest in the other's thoughts and feelings and is likely to establish rapport, if listening happens with an open mind.

Invitation to reflect
- What is your experience with appraisal meetings (as a super-/sub-ordinate)?
- Are the two conversation partners meeting on eye-level? Explain your response.
  - If yes: In your view, how is meeting at eye level established in the scenario?
  - If no: What is it that stands in the ways of meeting at eye level?
- Are you aware of any situation in which you'd better avoid meeting the other at eye level? If so, can you characterize such situations?

Insight
In management situations, there exist settings and means to facilitate meeting the other at eye level, if this is what you intend to.

Potential strategies
Decide consciously whether you aim for meeting the other at eye level.

Try to enjoy the learning that honest feedback by another can make possible.

Our insights

Meeting at eye level can be a profound, often kind of magical experience. It allows persons to grow in relationship to one another and to collaborate on solving challenging tasks in often creative, unorthodox ways.

Meeting at eye level entails risk, too. There is no pedestal from which you speak, there is no distance you put between yourself and the other person – the meeting is real, at face-value. But this is exactly what allows for genuine, uncomplicated sharing and builds trust. Whatever one's solution, resolution or goal is, meeting at eye level will tend to bring it about faster and more candidly.

Where eyes meet in respect and a positive attitude towards each other is given, synergy is born.

Next steps to competencies

Do some of the following ideas make sense to you?

- Organization
  - When serving in a supervisory role, meet your employees at eye-level and be accessible at least at certain times.
  - Allow for a culture that welcomes meeting at eye level by providing room(s), time, and events for facilitating contact.
  - Meet your customers at eye level by listening to them and including them in activities.

- Team
  - Practice openly listening to your colleagues, super- and sub-ordinates. See the world through their eyes too. This gives you a bigger picture. Moreover, it tends to be a way to motivate them to reciprocate your behavior and to establish a respectful, open climate in your team and even organization.

- Individual
  - Reflect on conversations and your feelings resulting from them.
  - Be aware that the other is a human being exactly as you are.

Final reflections

Do you agree?
- If you do not experience moments of meeting at least from time to time, you don't live your life fully.
- In every person there is something that I can learn from him or her.
- "I don't erect towers, I build bridges." Martin Buber

References

Czech (2011). *Komunikace zaměřená na člověka*. Praha: Grada; in English (2014). *Person-centred communication*. UK: McGrawHill.
dosSantos, A. (2003). *Miracle moments*. New York: iUniverse.
Motschnig, R., & Nykl, L. (2009). *Konstruktive Kommunikation*. Stuttgart: Klettt-Cotta.
Rogers, C. R. (1961). *On becoming a person*. USA: Houghton Mifflin Company.
Rogers, C.R., & Farson, R. E. (1987). *Active listening. Communicating in Business Today*. Online: http://www.gordontraining.com/pdf/active_listening_article_rogers-farson.pdf.
Senge, P. M. (2006). *The fifth discipline: The art & practice of the learning organization*. USA: Currency Doubleday.

Hiding consumes energy: Untie and focus

Hiding means consciously concealing some important information or feelings relevant to a process involving (or requiring) collaboration with others. It may have different causes like mistrust, fear, uncertainty, manipulation or other hidden agenda targeted to reach different goals than the common ones. Hiding not only consumes productive energy, but can also be costly. In practice, managers may face major consequences when not being transparent:

1) **If information or personal motivations are hidden, trust between people and within teams will decrease.** This lack of trust will influence other aspects of cooperation between individuals or departments.
2) **This leads to lower productivity as the flow is hampered** (see also: "*Transparency yields flow*"): As hiding consumes energy in interactions, less energy can be used productively for reaching project goals.
3) **Learning within the team will be blocked** due to misunderstandings.
4) When cooperation is not effective and people cannot learn from each other, **costs will increase.**

This moreover applies on an **intrapersonal level. Goals we have not reached yet concern us, even if we are involved in different processes.** If the environment is not suitable to reveal our inner concerns (see also: "*Care for the atmosphere*") – be it rivalry with a co-worker, anger due to uncommunicated decisions of the leader, or lovesickness – we accept or prefer to tuck away what truly concerns us.

Hiding interferes with transparency – something that is potentially visible or on your mind needs to be concealed by investing some effort. If I need to take care not to say something, this adds cognitive emotional load and consumes limited mental resources. **Of course it would be naive to reveal sensitive data, therefore a conscious decision as what to hide and what to reveal is necessary.**

So why do people hide information or feelings?

Obviously, revealing our issues may be threatening. Hiding information or personal motivation in negotiation situations or leadership positions might be perceived as a way to ensure power and be respected by employees. But the opposite strategy is more sustainable: creating an open and trustful communication basis with employees, customers, or stakeholders. This may be more time-consuming in short-term, but helps a team or company to generate a competitive advantage in the long-term, especially in terms of lower turnover and more creative ideas. Building trust with customers or within the team is challenging – it demands some risk-taking in the first place and a change of your own mindset, but you will be surprised how far this will get you. When the environment allows people to share openly, it takes a lot of weight out of situations or concerns, and we can follow our inner motivation more easily.

Some questions about hiding in the context of management you might ask are:

- What risks versus benefits are there for each piece of information that is hidden/revealed?
- What, in the worst case, can happen if some piece of information will become public?
- How can I assure the proper level of privacy and publicity?
- Could more transparency be valued by clients/colleagues or would it pose some hindrance?

Keywords: Lack of transparency/openness avoidance of communication, rigid decision-making, honest communication and contracting.

Cases

Overview of cases

- The first case **"Inform your subordinates 5 minutes before a strategic meeting"** shows how a lack of transparency and communication affects the work atmosphere. And it is well known that a good working climate positively impacts creativity and productivity.

- The second case **"Contracting in ICT-consulting projects"** illustrates an example of how being transparent even in difficult settings, such as negotiations, can be beneficial.

Case 1:
Inform your subordinates 5 minutes before a strategic meeting

Keywords: lack of transparency, avoidance of communication, avoidance of interference, rigid decision-making.

Situation
This case illustrates an organizational change in a large project team. As new executives were hired, resources for administrative tasks had to be reallocated. Top management worked out a model that regulated the share of administrative support per executive.

Scenario
Since it was clear that all executive team members would need administrative support, they talked a lot about possible shifts and solutions. Some presented plans for optimal reallocations to the top management board. The board did not respond to suggestions. Only a direct inquiry to one of the top executives brought kind of a response:

ExecTM: Executive Team Member   *TopMgr*: Top Management

ExecTM: "May I have your attention for a while? (TopMgr nods) You know, there's a lot of disturbance among employees, some feel unsure where and for whom they'll be working in the near future— some are even considering leaving. Couldn't we just sit together and talk and make a plan? That would be very helpful for all concerned."

TopMgr: "There's no need to worry. We are going to resolve this once the new people are here. I don't want to do it without them."

ExecTM: "Okay, I see. And good we don't need to worry."

After some time, the top management board called the executive team members for a brief meeting that was going to start minutes before an important strategic meeting in which the reallocations were to be formally announced. In that minute long meeting, new reallocation plans were presented as thoroughly elaborated *win-win solutions*, meeting the wishes of the administrative and executive staff. The only problem was, that some executive team members lost more than half of their administrative support. The meeting was over once the announcement was presented and argued and the formal meeting started.

Comment

Presented reallocations were well thought through and perhaps close to the best that could have been achieved under the given circumstances. Maybe, they would have been (very close to) the result of sitting together and talking beforehand. However, the whole process, including the way they were announced, left a deeply negative impression on employees. They experienced that social ties would be ignored and their views would count only in so far as they fit those of the top management of the organization. They were not invited to co-frame a solution. Instead of constructive talk beforehand – that surely would have consumed working time – there was complaint afterwards that not only consumed working time but led to a perceivable decline in the work climate and morale. Employees explained that they are reminded of that strategic action each time they see a living reminder of it, and this happens quite often.

Invitation to reflect
- How do you perceive the course of action of the top management board? What would you have done if you were part of it?
- Should the executive employees have acted differently?
- Knowing that negative emotions are counterproductive, what would you – as one of the concerned persons – do to work through them or put them aside?

Insights
Even the best top solution may be criticized if people who are concerned aren't part of it, don't get a choice, and the solution is imposed by an order.

If important decisions from the top are available, work can go on. Energy can be put into more complex work again.

Organizations are (also) social constructions.

Transparency and internal communication cost time and effort, but there is no doubt that they improve the work climate if done effectively.

Potential strategies
Involve people or – at least – inform employees as early as possible in management decisions. This may also mean to invest time in the decision-making and information sharing process, but helps to improve the work climate and create a more effective environment.

Case 2:
Contracting in ICT-consulting projects

Keywords: transparency, openness, honest communication and contracting.

Situation
In a SME, which collaborated with the iCom team, honest realistic negotiations were sought for. Compared to many big consulting houses, work relationships were founded on a personal level.

Scenario
In a classic negotiation situation party A (suppliers) and party B (customer) would both calculate their budgets. For the negotiation situations, party A would add up a specific amount, while party B would reduce their budget. During the negotiations, when prices are discussed, both will stick to their unrealistic prices and will meet somewhere in the middle in the end. Creating a consensus is not the problem; rather the unrealistic, "false" negotiation basis creates a lot of tension. Moreover, there is no transparency from both sides how prices are estimated and calculated. Consequently, there will be no trust between the parties, which may also affect their further cooperation.

The SME in this case decided to break this cycle and decided to be very accurate, realistic and transparent in their negotiations and actually name the amount of money they really needed. Party A was actively open towards party B: they revealed their realistic price calculations (not higher prices), were very trustful that party B won't negotiate the transparent price settings, and they did not hide their intensions. What were the effects of this change?
- As there was more trust between the parties, the relationships improved and made negotiations a lot easier.
- As a consequence, in a short-term resources and energy invested in the negotiations could be reduced.
- In long-term, customers stuck longer with the company, as trust and better relationships were created.
- Party A's behavior also affected Party B – there was no wall to hide information anymore, but rather an unconstrained flow of information.

In addition, face-to-face contact with the client and regular feedback got more important to be able to meet at eye level and built up trust.

Comment
On the one hand, being very transparent and open makes you vulnerable. But more importantly, openness creates trust and better relationships. Such trust building, especially in tricky business situations, creates valuable benefits in the long-term: higher binding of customers, fewer hours for negotiations, more satisfaction on both – customer and supplier – sides.

> **Invitation to reflect**
> - How are you negotiating with your customers or your suppliers? Which strategy do you follow? How satisfying are your negotiations?
> - In which negotiation situations is it easy for you to be open? In what situations is it important for you to hide bits of information?
> - Could you imagine trying to be more transparent in your pricing/ more honest about your actual budget?

Insights
Openness and transparency feel risky in the first attempt, but can generate fewer risks in the future. Also, hiding information is even more blocking – and therefore a higher risk – to trust and long-lasting relationships.

Being transparent and open does not mean giving always all information. However, being transparent in all aspects relevant to the problem is the key. Definitely, you need to adapt the depth of transparency to the situation. Still, in the long-term we are convinced that honesty and transparency will be rewarded by most customers.

Our insights

Hiding information (e.g. new business facts) and motivations (e.g. personal agenda), as threatening as they might appear, consumes energy – work energy, but also personal energy and team energy. On a personal level, hiding drains energy as additional effort is needed to maintain what we want to keep hidden, be it through lies, denial of facts or other strategies. In work, hiding generates a vicious cycle: lower level trust, hindered flow and team cooperation, more conflicts, and a downwards spiral in productivity and effectiveness. Having the feeling that decisions and information are not shared, creates a negative impression among employees and affects their work motivation (compare Case 1). On the other hand, being very transparent and open in making vital decisions – such as in contracting situations (compare Case 2) – creates trust and builds sustainable relationships between cooperating partners. And the energy needed for hiding can be used for relevant tasks as well as building personal relationships. Still, you need to adapt to the given situation: if openness and transparency are one-way-attitudes rather than reciprocal, you may need to accept that this approach is not possible with a communication partner.

Next steps to competencies

Make a conscious decision about how transparent you want to be in your work environment and consider:

- Organization
  - Establish a working culture that is rather threat free, failure tolerant, and where management decisions and intentions are shared openly. (See also: "Care for the atmosphere")

- Team
  - Sharing information does not mean losing power. Rather, you will receive more and better-quality information from your team if you sincerely share yourself. (See also: "Transparency yields flow")

- Individual
    - Making mistakes and communicating them openly – instead of pretending to be perfect – will create respect. If leaders openly reflect on their personal challenges, mistakes, employees and the whole organization can learn from that experience and your team may appreciate your honesty and openness! It might even inspire your employees to try new things without fearing failure.

Final reflections

In what ways do you agree with these statements?

Good, effective cooperation needs:
- 'Real', honest sharing.
- Open & transparent as well as frequent (face-to-face) communication.
- Socially competent leaders: persons who can build trust with teams and towards stakeholders by understanding their needs and motivations, who can adapt to difficult situations, and who have an open and honest attitude in business cooperation.
- A specific mindset: mistakes are no weaknesses, but potential to learn (for everybody in the organization).

Further resources:

Ryback, D. (1998): *Putting emotional intelligence to work: successful leadership is more than IQ.* Boston: Butterworth-Heinemann.
This book illustrates why honesty and trust are so essential for cooperating in teams.

More Agility through Technology

Maximize the chance for success: Be agile

Nowadays, high competition, dynamic changes of markets and technologies, wide Internet adoption, and the velocity of the development process have become some of the most important success criteria for projects. Traditional project management models have become inadequate for the new business demands. In contrast, quick, flexible, adaptive processes together with creative designs have become highly valuable for the success of innovative projects.

One key problem of traditional concepts is their bureaucratic burden. The majority of classic methods rely on the client's ability to clearly and holistically define requirements in the beginning of a project. After the definition phase, requirements cannot be adapted and later changes lead to tension between customer and the project manager as well as within the team. Additionally, people often get used to rigid aspects and processes in projects – including all project management phases – and start resisting changes. The fear of facing areas they are not familiar with decreases their motivation for trying out something different or new. Many decision makers – independently of business structures and size – may often not be aware of these approaches and preserve traditional approaches, which might not be the most beneficial choice.

Agile approaches, in contrast, may support solving these aspects and may increase the chance for being successful in projects. Several approaches – among which Scrum (Schwaber, 2004) might be most spread – provide guidelines on how to build agile teams. Despite the origin in software development, agile methodologies are applicable in many other areas aside programming such as marketing, logistics, or even for creating a book (see also: "Introduction"). Still, all methods follow the same underlying principles: a high focus on the product and its quality, short release cycles and frequent reviews, emphasis on customer collaboration, continuous learning, informal knowledge sharing, and participative decision-making.

Many managers are counting on highly structured processes for large, high-complexity projects while preferring agile processes for smaller teams. Contrary to this opinion, large projects can be divided into smaller parts where agile approaches can be easily applied. These smaller parts of huge projects are much more controllable and adjustable. **The flexibility you may gain helps you to adapt the outcome to current needs and reflect latest changes, especially regarding customers' expectations.** Agile methodologies offer several advantages such as higher end-user involvement throughout the process – though, agility alone does not ensure the overall success of particular projects. As the environment is changing dynamically and competition increases in every business area, strict validation in the initiation phase – when the idea and project vision is born – is required. **This implies frequent contact and dialogue with the customer and future potential users to ensure you are on the right track.** The modern approach of "Lean Start-Up" by Eric Ries (2011) – combining agile/iterative processes and a focus on business-driven validation – helps to minimize losses and to validate the idea by adjusting the outcome for the targeted audience in the very beginning. This model is suitable for projects regardless of type – whether for start-ups, small business, or initiatives within large corporations.

The application of agile procedures in organizations remains problematic. Incorrect grasp of being agile (for example lack of acceptance, organizational change, or empowering people as well as insufficient trust, missing communication and team skills, or incomplete application of agile processes) creates needless tension in the team and organization, discontinues important innovations, and neutralizes positive effects of agile procedures.

So, what processes are there in your sphere of influence that might benefit from a lean or agile strategy? Do you think that managers working with lean or agile approaches need other skills and attitudes than managers working with classical approaches? If so, what skills and attitudes are needed, in particular, and how could they be developed in junior managers and team members?

Keywords: Agile, lean, business, development, customer, feedback, cost reduction, user, experience, success.

Cases

Overview of cases

The three cases examine significant aspects of agility in project teams from interacting with customers on requirements to adapting business processes for more flexibility.

- The first case **"Get clients involved"** discusses how to involve client's expertise in the development process by appreciating their views and knowledge. This case also shows the positive effects of direct communication with the customer, frequent feedback loops, and personal relationships.

- The second case **"Starting to be agile"** illustrates how organizations could start following agile management principles and exemplifies that an open attitude towards agile principles may help to change work habits towards agile work procedures.

- Finally, the third case **"Learning the price of time – Implementing lean principles"** is about adapting quickly, validating cheaply and saving costs through lean management strategies in a start-up company.

Case 1:
Get clients involved

Keywords: Person-product-profit, listening, learning together, meeting at eye level, inclusion, getting closer.

Situation
The case of Kentico demonstrates how a SME works very closely with their clients and involves them in every stage of the project process. Further, it highlights the fact that the client's views are highly appreciated by Kentico (the developers and project managers) and how that has led to close and good relationships with the clients.

Scenario

Kentico, a Czech SME specialized on software development, is a best-practice example for tight and participative customer collaboration. To achieve this close collaboration, the company applies three agile principles in their daily work: direct communication, appreciating and encouraging frequent feedback, and emphasizing transparency to build and maintain personal relationships with the customers.

Direct communication with the customer

Cooperating and communicating as direct as possible is key – preferably face-to-face. Kentico discovered that their project results – outcomes such as services, new products, or innovation – are far better if they visit their partners in the region regularly. A Kentico manager stated: *"Getting feedback online is very hard – mainly you will receive either none or very simple answers (e.g., just yes or no), but no real insights. It is much easier to contact the customer directly in person, or meet them at their location. When you visit your customers for a few days, you can talk more direct about their problems or watch how they work."*

Often, barriers between departments – even within one company – hinder feedback. At Kentico, developers experienced that feedback got lost, as the customer care department was responsible for the communication between developers and customers. In some cases, the customers' feedback never reached the developers. Given these circumstances, Kentico decided to get all involved people from the care department and the customer directly together with the development teams. Through this measure, the relevant players are co-located and consequently, feedback is more direct.

Encouraging frequent feedback and emphasizing transparency

Kentico clearly benefits from the customers' involvement by receiving quick feedback. On the one hand, this feedback enables them to learn. *"If you are working with somebody invisible or untouchable it is really hard to work on things. In contrast, if you see if the customer is satisfied or directly elaborate issues, it is easier to cooperate"*, the Kentico manager explains. Such direct feedback reveals valuable information on how the product is applied as well as on motives and need to initiate a project. This helps the developers to understand what is actually needed and influences the productivity and effectiveness of the developers.

On the other hand, the customer benefits equally. First, the customer has more influence on shaping the product, will get a better outcome in the end, and consequently be more satisfied – as she or he gets what is really needed. Second, through frequent contact with Kentico, the partners get an insight into their supplier. This is especially important in the ICT-world where partners can feel easily anxious when new changes arise or situations get uncertain. The manager explains: *"Customers like Kentico as a company and the product for several reasons. We try to be always open and we fix whole issues within days. Customers can also see from the outside how Kentico's internal culture looks like. Everybody at Kentico feels really as part of the company and if somebody is so engaged about the company, then the customers might feel that the product is the same – made with love."*

Transparent, personal relationships with the customers

The company Kentico has a primary focus on personal relationships with their customers. Therefore, personal meetings (at least once a year) are extremely important as they enable the customer to feel closer to the company and facilitate effective cooperation. *"If you want to understand the customer, you should know them in person. The personal contact is necessary."* One of the key aspects of Kentico's success is that its employees are really trying to listen to what the customer says and to create an understanding for what is really wanted. This care for the customer starts in the initiation phase and lasts throughout the entire project duration. Throughout the project people at Kentico are always willing to help the customers, solve their problems and – maybe most importantly – appreciate every customer's perspective and ideas. This behavior towards the customer has very positive effects for the company: most customers stay with Kentico for years.

> **Invitation to reflect**
> - How would you describe the relationships you have with your clients/students/co-workers?
> - How do you get customers/students/co-workers to give feedback or give information?
> - In which ways are the clients'/students'/co-workers' perspectives appreciated?
> - Are the clients'/co-workers' perspectives ignored sometimes and on what basis? What effect does this tend to have?

Insights

Keeping the customer's benefits in mind and taking care of the mutual success of the project together with the customer helps Kentico to motivate clients to cooperate by giving feedback and supplying information.

Clients are able to share more easily, if you sit and talk with them. Having close contact with the client often ends up in broader relationships enabling clients to get help or insight also in various areas. This eventually leads to an increase of value of the business relationship itself. The relationship has to be built from the very beginning and it does not end with the product delivery. Gathering feedback throughout the cooperation and openly sharing ideas and problems helps to build trustful relationships that last for years.

Close relationships with customers and receiving their feedback as soon as possible enables to adapt to changing environmental conditions flexibly.

Case 2:
Starting to be agile

Keywords: Agile application, transition difficulties, workplace culture change, Scrum.

Situation

The application of agile processes needs to be a part of a company's culture. This case provides two examples – one of the company Kentico; another of a start-up 'Takeplace', trying to find its place in the market. Both examples illustrate how the implementation of agile principles proceeded and led to an overall improvement in customer satisfaction. Further, they show the effect of less tension between teams within the organization.

Scenario A

The Czech SME Kentico started to change towards agile development three years ago. Unlike many would expect this change was not a business-driven decision, but a bottom-up change. The first impulses came from the employees who had read articles on agile development and wanted to try this procedure in their projects. The top management supported the employees' attempts from the first minute. Why? – *"Because agile approaches allow Kentico to adapt to market changes!"* After three years it became a top priority for the whole company. This is for sure supported by the public visibility and the fact that the top management also reinforced the change.

At the stage of implementation, Kentico counted approximately 80 employees. In larger companies such changes are way more difficult: Bottom-up decisions usually do not work that well. Often, organizations are not succeeding to change towards agile, but end up in workarounds. For example: teams may meet on a daily basis as the agile methods suggest – and that can help to communicate – but other aspects of agility are not applied.

Another critical point for Kentico was the role of a product owner – the person who represents the customer's needs and expectations and works on a daily basis with the development team. As agile approaches are highly business-driven, this role needs to have a clear vision, needs to be able to present the ideas and to really represent the customer, and finally needs to know what the market needs and communicate that to the whole team. In practice, it is not always likely to obtain such a skilled person.

Scenario B

The start-up company 'Takeplace', which develops technical facilitation tools for organizing events, experimented with several different approaches before deciding to develop in an agile manner.

First, they applied sequential software development methods (such as the waterfall approach), but the company quickly experienced some downsides, especially high costs for testing and maintenance. Consequently, Takeplace decided to apply a Scrum process (Schwaber and Beedle, 2001). "*As developers are in daily contact with the customer, they ensure the users' involvement in the development process, provide feedback, and communicate within the team what customers expect in the next release cycle*", Josef Hubr (CTO) stated. Using collaborative tools that helped tracking the production and testing steps supported this process.

Apart from technical support, the agile process was supported by a particular management approach. This did not only include lean organizational structures, but also a strong common vision and strategy that were well communicated, as well as a certain type of leadership: decisions were made in cooperation and communication is highly supported by the organization.

> **Invitation to reflect**
> - Is the situation in your organization similar to one of the two examples in this case?
> - How would you apply a new approach in your company? Which restraints may be there for you?

Insights

Agile approaches are widely accepted by co-workers, but might not be suitable for everybody. Still, many like working in agile-oriented companies as agility can help to facilitate cooperating with others in a respectful, regardful way.

Changing organizational processes will be more likely to succeed if the employees recognize and feel the need for this change.

Agile adaptation and incorporation in the organization is a crucial moment that often leads to the point people around will resign and say that this cannot be changed. Therefore, the implementation of agile approaches needs careful preparation, attention, and supervision.

Case 3:
Learning the price of time – Implementing lean principles

Keywords: Lean, business, idea, validation, customer, satisfaction, experience.

Situation

Steering your company effectively is a challenging task for every leader. The iCom team had many chances to discuss among managers how they create company strategies. Some of the managers from companies and institutions we met during the iCom project had real-life experience with the lean approach popular inspired by Eric Ries' (2011) approach of 'Lean Start-Ups' and Ash Mauraya's 'Running Lean' (2012).

A lean approach can help start-up companies – but also traditional companies – to achieve great results. It allows effectively handling and validating new ideas with unparalleled speed and effectiveness. This may lead to innovation bringing high value to the customer. Launching a new project or building a new company has always been a set of more or less difficult tasks accompanied with lots of documents. You often write a project proposal, requirements, analyzes of the current situation, assemble a team, and start producing the outcome. And somewhere in this sequence of events, you may find out that something went wrong. The environment has changed, clients refuse the outcome, or you realize that the investment for the project will not create the revenues you expected.

Customers are asked about product features, pricing, distribution channels, and customer acquisition strategies. An emphasis lies on performing this validation as soon and frequent as possible: After achieving a first minimal viable product (a project outcome in a minimal version able to represent a minimal set of fundamental expectations), another iteration of getting feedback from customers begins.

Scenario

During the iCom project, participants of the company "Celebrio Software" shared their experiences with the application of lean principles:

"*We have started as a company based on an idea which we felt so passionate about that we have begun writing code right from the beginning without any true validation. First tests were made after three months when we showed potential users some prototypes and ideas to make sure that everything is clear enough for them to understand and use*", a manager of the company described. Initial product development involved in the beginning more guessing what the customer might like than a grounded strategy. This fact makes validation so important when developing a product. The representative of Celebrio Software added, "*Based on lean principles we should have validated the idea from the very beginning long before writing any actual code. The first step to take is to get to know whether users even care. Create some landing page and watch how many users and friends will sign up. Ask people around you about their opinion. Never ask whether they like your solution but once they confirm they have the problem you are trying to solve, begin by asking how they would prefer it to be solved*". Here is an example: if you are developing software for sharing files, you would start by asking friends what applications they already use to share their data, what they like about them and what they would improve. If problems emerge you would ask how they wish the problem to be solved and whether they have tried to look for a solution and how. This way helps to get to know where to get inspiration for the project outcome, what to avoid and what to solve and validate and if there even is any problem worth solving. Every new hypothesis or idea that emerges would have to be validated by the same process.

> **Invitation to reflect**
> - Can you imagine a start of the project with the client advising a lean validation first, having in mind his/her own good?

Insights

In early stages validation helps to prove how accurate your guesses are. Therefore, validate as early as possible – but also be prepared that validation may also reveal that you are not on the right track. Still, no validation would mean a potential waste of time and resources working on something that is not needed.

Validating in lean management means understanding – understanding market's demands, customer's needs, and client's issues.

Lean validation implies intensive communication: you have to do expert interviews (= communicating) with end-users, doing various surveys (specific kind of communication). You need to communicate your intension already in vision phase, which is often not very easy (you are clarifying your vision at that time).

Our insights

Agile procedures help to reach customers faster, controlling the project course with very minor corrections when issues arise – instead of waiting a few weeks to get milestones done and make major adjustments thereafter. Through agile principles, work can be reduced as you only perform tasks that are actually needed. Further, the key stakeholders should be tightly involved – e.g., meeting every 3 days or once a week instead of meeting once a month or every two months. Inquiries may increase in these aspects. What usually would take up to several months in traditional processes, can be reduced in terms of time. Implementing a lightweight development process helps eliminating bottlenecks, reducing overheads and making the process more efficient and result-driven.

Agile management describes processes, but equally involves essential attitudes and behaviors in cooperation and communication. Among others, direct communication, open and frequent feedback, and building personal relationships are vital. Especially Case 1 illustrates how an agile development process needs to be supported by these principles, and how it helps to be innovative, more effective, and create sustainable partnerships.

Agile approaches are not only applicable in technical areas such as software development. During the iCom project, we engaged in various fields of application such as marketing, event management, or – last but not least – in book development (see *"Introduction"*).

Next steps to competencies

Make a conscious decision about how transparent you want to be in your work environment and consider:

- Organization
  - Validate from the very beginning. Customers' involvement ensures you more precise outcomes according to their expectation and the overall satisfaction in your team increases.

- Team
  - Listening is the key – listening to the client's needs, listening to the members of the team.
  - Adapt as soon as possible. The later you recognize the environment has changed the more costs the project will require.

- Individual
  - Take time before deciding to change – not every project is suitable for an agile approach.

Final reflections

In what ways do you agree with these statements?
- Being agile is not a dogma.
- Some authors swear on well-structured processes for large, high-complexity projects and prefer agile ones for smaller teams. Depending on the project, it is sometimes better to be plan-oriented and sometimes to be agile. It depends on the particular situation, the specific project.
- The more technical devices and ICT enable fast contact anytime and anywhere, the more there's a tendency to be flexible or agile. Still, technical devices can't substitute for rich face-to-face communication, as agile approaches to management nicely confirm.

References

Maurya, A. (2012). *Running Lean: Iterate from Plan A to a Plan that Works (2nd ed.)*. Sebastopol, CA: O'Reilly.
Ries, E. (2011). *The Lean Startup: How Today's Entrepreneurs Use Continuous Innovation to Create Radically Successful Businesses*. New York: Crown Publishing.
Schwaber, K. (2004). *Agile Project Management with Scrum*. Redmond, WA: Microsoft Press.
Schwaber, K., & Beedle, M. (2001). *Agile Software Development with Scrum*. Upper Saddle River, NJ: Prentice Hall.

Further resources:
Kniberg, H. (2007). Scrum and XP from the Trenches. In E*nterprise Software Development Series*. InfoQ.
   A simple, practice-proven guideline to apply Scrum and XP in your projects.

VersionOne (2013). 7th Annual State of Agile Development Survey. VersionOne, Inc. http://www.versionone.com/pdf/7th-Annual-State-of-Agile-Development-Survey.pdf
   A survey on current trends in agile software development.

Two steps ahead

The **trends in ICT-development and the ICT-paradigm are changing.** According to Gartner (2013a) and IDC (2013a), in 2017 there will be twice as many tablets as PCs and they will become the primary ICT-Device. What does this mean for the understanding and utilization of ICT in business?

The general availability of remote collaborative tools built on cloud services **changes the way we communicate with both our friends and colleagues.** Similarly, 3D printing could change the way we are selling goods to our clients in both business-to-business and business-to-customer settings.

The Internet of Things is not a buzzword of the future. Look around and you will see plenty of devices already connected to the Internet sharing and exchanging data with other devices, making peoples' lives easier and more comfortable.

Utilization of ICT does not concern only experts or scientists anymore. ICT-devices became regular consumer goods; they are readily accessible and easy to use. A well-timed detection of interesting opportunities they brought about led not only to many innovative ideas; it also substantially improved communication between users, including companies and their customers.

On the other hand, the pervasiveness and ubiquity of the next-generation mobile technology brings problems that, only a couple of years ago, one could not even conceive. Nonetheless, we have to cope with them more and more often. The following cases illustrate a couple of them.

Keywords: Mobile, smartphones, tablets, trends, modern, technologies, adaptation, daily life, opportunities.

Cases

Overview of cases

- Case 1 **"Be ready for a changing ICT-paradigm"** sketches future ways of technology-supported communication drawing from current developments in mobile device markets.

- Case 2 **"Tablet or laptop?"** illustrates the perception of using modern ICT-devices in an international business meeting from the position of a participant.

- Case 3 **"Two sides of a coin"** describes changes in business processes and management due to the use of modern ICT-devices.

Case 1:
Be ready for a changing ICT-paradigm

Keywords: Mobile platforms, trends, paradigm, ICT-utilization.

Here are some impressions of the influence of new technologies in communication by a member of the iCom team:

"Nowadays, the tablet market is one of the most rapidly growing branches producing hundreds of millions of tablets every year. These devices redefine communication methods not only in the consumer segments but also in business environments. They help to change the way people communicate and collaborate anywhere and anytime. Are modern mobile devices just a fashion trend or do they bring about a real change that is going to influence the way we use ICT-technologies in future decades?

The research vice-president at Gartner, Carolina Milanesi, reported their findings from the Gartner's market research reflecting a significant shift in the way people want to interact with technology. Gartner (2013b) states, *"Consumers want anytime-anywhere computing that allows them to consume and create content with ease, but also share and access that content from a different portfolio of products* (Business Insider, 2013)".

Tablets are turning into essential business tools due to their natural mobility and the fact that they are very easy to use. People have become fond of them because of a set of innovative features and functionalities they brought into the enterprise sector. These are, for example, instant access, availability of thousands of collaborative and productivity applications, access to content anytime and anywhere, and an all-inclusive user experience.

Using mobile, visual and social communication technologies makes it easier to work anytime and anywhere. The next-generation enterprise applications, which offer a uniform way of communication and collaboration, will allow co-workers to be accessible from any place and round-the-clock. Incorporating real-time collaboration tools into the organizational workflow becomes even more important as, according to Gartner and IDC researchers (Gartner, 2013c; IDC, 2013b; Gartner, 2013d), tablets will become primary ICT-devices within the next 5 years.

New ways of communication that are already common in the consumer segment, such as video chat, are now enhanced by virtual workplaces which enable people to work from home more than ever before. New communication technologies are immediate, interactive, and result in an enhancement of interpersonal communication.

Tablets are more and more acknowledged for making collaboration easier and one day may replace PC and videoconference systems as the preferred way of communication."

Invitation to reflect
- Do you consider a tablet to be a device you could use all the time as your primary IT tool?
- Are you willing to adapt to the different ICT-utilization workflows if modern mobile devices will bring you more flexibility and freedom in accessing data?
- Is a big reason for avoiding modern mobile devices such as tablets or wearable smart devices as a business tool you being unfamiliar with the possibilities they offer – or – unwillingness to change your routines?

Insights

The amount of data we are consuming every day is increasing rapidly. Modern devices can accommodate the need for selecting the right pieces of information. However, as it is a relatively new concept and ICT-approach, users may have to overcome some prejudices towards such devices.

Case 2:
Tablet or Laptop?

Keywords: Project meeting, laptop, tablet, contact, barrier.

Situation

An international project team presented their results at a review meeting with the European Commission. After the results of each work-package had been presented, three reviewers asked questions and provided immediate feedback. Written feedback was also expected later on.

Scenario

Interestingly, while all the three reviewers made an honest effort to provide useful and constructive feedback, the ways they interacted with the project team were different. Let us take a closer look at them:

The first reviewer, a woman in her fifties, appeared to be busy fidgeting with her laptop. She was almost hidden behind its large screen and only rarely asked a question or interacted with the audience. Just once during the whole one-day meeting she engaged in a longer interaction with the audience on the use of media by young people. While sharing on this topic, she pushed her laptop aside and almost closed the screen. She used her arms to gracefully underline her arguments and signal her engagement. This was the only time during the presentation part of the meeting when she spoke to the team as a person. Only from that time on she became really present and the team's trust in her rose. Before that, team members (as was reflected in a meeting afterwards) were not sure about her, uncertain whether they can trust her, and what they should expect from her in the written report.

The second reviewer, a young woman, occasionally took notes on her small laptop. She was in charge of the review meeting and even though her laptop was placed in front of her and at times it caught her attention, she seemed to be in contact with the participants (team and reviewers) the vast majority of time. The screen of her laptop was almost at level with the desk and so she remained unobstructed and clearly visible all the time. We felt safe and respected during the whole meeting.

Finally, the third reviewer, a young man, had a tablet to occasionally take notes on. He appeared to be the one who – intuitively – we found highly sympathetic and trustful. He was a perfect listener. He maintained eye-contact with the audience for almost the whole time. Even when taking notes, he seemed to be doing it almost "automatically", still keeping one of his "attention channels" open for the audience. Though he didn't talk much, whenever he said something it was perfectly justified and to the point.

Comment

Review meetings tend to be rather complex since they deal with various tasks and responsibilities. The scenario was meant to illustrate the reciprocal influence of the usage of electronic devices and styles of interaction from the point of view of a "consumer". Fortunately, modern technology gives us a wide range of choices of ever better electronic devices. However, being *two steps ahead* means not only to possess an appropriate device but also to be able to use it smoothly, thoughtfully, and in response to a particular situation.

Invitation to reflect
- What is your experience with using electronic devices in meetings? What is your opinion on how other people use laptops, tablets, and smartphones in meetings?
- Do you think that tablets allow for better contact in meetings than laptops?
- Do you think that people should acquire competence with using electronic devices in meetings? If so, how, in your view, could such training be provided and/or organized?

Potential strategies
Observe others and consciously reflect on the cost and the merit of using electronic devices in meetings.

Reflect your views, experiences and feelings concerning the use of tablets (other devices) in your team and try to improve your meeting atmosphere as well as your organization's efficiency.

Case 3:
Two sides of a coin

Keywords: Mobile platforms, trends, paradigm, ICT-utilization.

Situation
The increasing utilization of mobile devices, especially those brought by employees themselves (BYOD – Bring Your Own Device), requires a complex change of organization and ICT-infrastructure. Nevertheless, does it change the overall key performance indicators?

Scenario
Securing employee-owned devices and supporting different mobile platforms can present a source of complex problems for ICT-departments to deal with. The costs connected with customized software solutions, which allow for 100% utilization of mobile devices also has to be considered.

However, mobile devices can increase efficiency even in areas where one would not expect them to, at least not at first glance – e.g., energy surveillance. An international electricity distributor operating in the region of Central Europe recently decided to change the way the regular technicians' reports were carried out. Instead of having to fill in conventional paper forms, scanning them and sending them via e-mail (or bringing them in person) technicians write all the data into a tablet and transmit them to the headquarters in real time via a GSM network. The competitive advantage is obvious – less paperwork, faster outdoor data analysis, and of course, marketing – the customers see the distributor as being rather progressive and in sync with the latest technology. Besides buying the actual tablets, the implementation of this new technology also includes designing special server applications, which manage communication with the tablets and store the data on the servers.

One of the iCom team members has seven years of experience in the area of event management including organizing outstanding events for the European Commission. This rather conservative area has undergone dramatic changes concerning the way things were dealt with. An event manager has to be very flexible, stress resistant, and also "on the move" almost all the time. He or she has to inspect event venues, negotiate catering and other services or discuss the program with speakers; an event manager only reaches his office at the end of his workday. Within the last four years, new services and applications built primarily for tablets and smartphones, goal of which is to provide a complex mobile tool covering all phases of organizing an event, have been introduced to the market. Event managers have access to all data relevant to the event; they are conveniently stored in a cloud. This set of tools has been designed primarily to master the event in the most efficient way; it enables for example budget control, program making, or managing payments directly on the tablets within one simple user interface. The obvious boundaries a personal computer in your office or a laptop has are eliminated thanks to the flexibility and immediate availability of mobile devices. Also from the perspective of participants, utilization of modern mobile devices during the event enhances their experience and engagement in the event itself. The situation of event managers is becoming easier while people adopt the recent technology in their daily life. Augmented reality and NFC (near field communication) became understandable and usable not only by the group of experts or early adopters but also by the general public. What would you do with these technologies as a company's event manager or an attendee? Imagine a set of applications unobtrusively motivating you to answer surveys concerning service/product and providing a significant amount of usable feedback – simply by using the tiny device you have in your pocket at all times. Everything should aim at satisfying your event attendees and communicating the company's message in a memorable way that will prevent them from forgetting it just moments later. What does it all mean regarding event management? You can register for the event from your favorite café, you can get information about other attendees in real time, and you can use a quick check-in. And there are certainly many more things to come.

> **Invitation to reflect**
> - Can you imagine having a part of your information system, a particular business workflow or a specific organizational process driven by modern mobile devices, such as tablets or smartphones? Which ones?
> - Do you see the future utilization of mobile devices as a necessary step to maintain innovation and sustainable organization's development?

Our insights

Tablets change the way people communicate and collaborate.

If tablets do not replace PCs in the end, they will certainly boost our everyday collaboration and interaction with other people.

We can expect the modern way of communication supported by the ubiquity of tablets to radically change our everyday lives.

Next steps to competencies

Do some of the following ideas make sense to you?

- Organization
  - Support the IT maintenance of the employees' own devices by encouraging the Bring-Your-Own-Device concept and setting up processes ensuring free but secure access to the organization's intranet. It could eventually save costs for new facilities but also increase the efficiency and availability of employees.

- Team
  - Many mobile applications support collaborative work within a team. They offer different views and user interfaces for different roles and positions. Try to use also supported hardware devices, which can help you present the tablet's screen on a TV or print it wirelessly.

- Personal
  - Tablets and smartphones are controlled in a slightly different way than conventional computers, focusing on one task at a time. Try to find applications that suit you best.

Final reflections

Do you agree?
- New ways of ICT usage and interaction will be introduced.
- The importance of mobile collaborative solutions will increase.
- More organizational agenda will be managed from mobile devices.

References

Business Insider (2013). *Tablet takeover to continue as Gartner forecasts 10 per cent decline in traditional PC sales.* 24/6/2013 http://www.businessinsider.com/pc-sales-to-plunge-again-2013-6

Gartner (2013a). *Worldwide PC, Tablet and Mobile Phone Shipments to Grow 4.5 Percent in 2013 as Lower-Priced Devices Drive Growth.* 21/10/2013 http://www.gartner.com/newsroom/id/2610015

Gartner (2013b). *Worldwide PC, Tablet and Mobile Phone Shipments to Grow 5.9 Percent in 2013 as Anytime-Anywhere-Computing Drives Buyer Behavior.* 24/6/2013 http://www.gartner.com/newsroom/id/2525515

Gartner (2013c). *Gartner Says by 2016, 70 Percent of the Most Profitable Companies Will Manage Their Business Processes Using Real-Time Predictive Analytics or Extreme Collaboration.* 26/2/2013 http://www.gartner.com/newsroom/id/2349215

Gartner (2013d). *Most Collaboration Applications Will Be Equally Available Across Multiple Devices by 2016.* 4/9/2013 http://www.gartner.com/newsroom/id/2584115

IDC (2013a). *Tablet Shipments Forecast to Top Total PC Shipments in the Fourth Quarter of 2013 and Annually by 2015.* 11/9/2013 http://www.idc.com/getdoc.jsp?containerId=prUS24314413

IDC (2013b). *Enterprise Social Networks and Collaborative Technologies.* http://www.idc.com/getdoc.jsp?containerId=IDC_P19643

Summary and Inspirations

Getting inspired

As you have now reached the last part of this book, we would like to share some final thoughts with you about potential applications within your work environment. After a summary of the major statements, we address lifelong learning questions like: How can you become a constructive communicator in practice? What could be your starting points for engaging in knowledge transfer activities with other companies and universities? Also, we develop some paths for transferring our project experiences to related fields such as secondary and higher education.

In addition to improving interpersonal communication and collaboration, we encourage companies to get in contact with higher education institutions and experience the benefits such working groups can bring along. Here, we will suggest some starting points for engaging in university-industry collaborations.

This book aims to inspire professional development and personal growth. In 13 topics, we tried to capture those aspects of communication in teams and organizations that we found to be most important. We elaborated our understanding of constructive communication in the work context with selected real case scenarios from ICT-businesses as well as the educational field (universities and schools). The situations described in the book are all somehow related to (direct as well as technology enhanced) communication. They are meant to encourage you to critically reconsider your personal interactions at work. We hope that you managed to transfer some of the described cases to your own situations and experiences. How would you have acted in a situation like those you read about? How do you deal with hardships in projects? What are your strategies in resolving interpersonal conflicts?

Summary and final remarks to the topics

The second chapter addresses different aspects of "KNOWLEDGE TRANSFER", meaning the creation of knowledge trough communication. When we use the expression "sharing or transferring knowledge", we refer to a complex process where information or experience is not only provided by someone and received by someone else. Knowledge cannot really be transferred; rather it is connected to previous knowledge and co-constructed within a certain context.

When we state that *knowledge grows from sharing*, we not only mean that more people have gained the same knowledge, but also that in the process of sharing it, new knowledge is generated. Every person involved in a process of knowledge sharing adds something new to the existing knowledge. Our project experiences have supported this view of knowledge creation. Active listening and open communication can therefore be regarded essential success factors within organizations.

As we see, learning means learning from others. In many cases, we develop new skills and knowledge by transferring concepts from one context to another and applying it there. Bringing people with different backgrounds together, having them exchange ideas can bring out the most elaborate and creative solutions. This is what we call *"Connect the dots"*. If you are open to accept totally different viewpoints and willing to scrutinize your own mental models, then you are on the right track to learn in connection with others. This is also a good starting point for engaging in cross-sector (e.g. between businesses and universities) and cross-cultural cooperation.

In Chapter 3 "LEARNING ORGANIZATION" we provided cases that show ways of putting learning processes in the heart of an organization. As a project team we also experienced what it means to learn and grow together. Among other things, we found that *"The team is the most wonderful place to learn"*. A team is a unique social construct. It is more than a few people working together, it entails the potential to learn from and develop alongside others. So, if you are part of a good working team, consider yourself lucky and actively contribute to a constructive team climate.

Making the right decisions by yourself might sometimes be hard. Making decisions as a team or as an organization – involving a higher number of people – will probably be even harder. *"Every perspective is valuable"* offered some experiences about how to come to satisfying solutions in teams. We found that while not every decision requires full basic-democratic discussions, impactful decisions should centrally involve the persons who are affected by it. In this sense, learning as an organization is also about learning how to create effective decision-making processes.

Transparency yields flow and provides energy for the things that are really important to you. Through various cases we illustrated how transparent communication can inspire and motivate project teams (i.e., how not being open can destroy good collaboration). Being open and transparent about personal agendas and explaining the real reasons for certain decisions is not appropriate in every situation and might sometimes not be possible.

Transparency requires courage, especially when the environment doesn't support open sharing.

In the chapter "LEADERSHIP" we showed various challenging situations where good leadership was crucial. The case studies proved that there is not one "correct" style of leading a team or organization; rather leadership requires a lot of flexibility. Being a good leader means to know when a team requires clear guidelines, specifications and goals that provide orientation and when, on the other hand, a team needs the most free space for creativity, self-organization and innovation.

To *hold constructs flexibly* refers to a kind of leadership that is adaptive to changing environments within and outside an organization. Strictly (or even blindly) following a plan without considering how a situation or a project develops is a form of leadership that belongs to a long gone past. Employees should be in the management's trust to stray from the planned track when circumstances require it. In such a trustful environment, employees carry more responsibility and are asked to critically reflect on their own and other's actions.

Enabling creativity in teams is about granting helpful freedom. This means freedom to experiment, to follow new unconventional paths and also to make mistakes. In an organization, developing creative teams is not only a strategic leadership task; everyone should contribute to it. An important starting point for developing creativity is finding out where the creative resources are: Discover, understand and foster your own creative potential, while at the same time being attentive to the strengths and weaknesses of your colleagues. It's important not to force someone to become a creative mind, but rather to motivate those who have a natural interest in creative thinking.

The *atmosphere* within a company essentially influences the performance of individuals, teams and the organization as a whole. Although the atmosphere might not be visible to us, it still defines how we can develop skills, enhance and share knowledge and collaborate with co-workers as well as external partners and clients. An organization's atmosphere is highly sensitive and small influences can have big effects – just like in a complex ecosystem. Therefore, every single person in a company contributes to the atmosphere and is responsible for keeping it growth-promoting.

CONSTRUCTIVE COMMUNICATION (chapter 5) means to follow some principles that allow for open and respectful communication. These three principles (congruence, unconditional positive regard and empathy) are defined in the Person-Centered Approach and they form the basic understanding of communication presented in this book.

Through our experiences we learnt that *communication matters* – no matter when and where. We agree that an organization exists primarily in the interactions of the people. Therefore, we can assume that a disturbed flow of communication must be a major threat to any organization. Communication flows have to be cultivated, even more in international collaborations where language is an additional stumbling block.

While hierarchies can destroy openness, *meeting at eye level opens doors*. Hierarchy exists in most organizations, though it might be more or less visible. Encountering another person at eye level doesn't mean to ignore hierarchy or authority, but rather to deal with it in a constructive and positive way. Being able to accept the knowledge, creativity and distinctiveness that lie in other persons make a constructive communicator (and hence a good project and team leader).

The topic *"Hiding consumes energy"* shows how obscure communication and hidden agendas can easily destroy trust. When people work in open environments where mistakes are accepted as valuable experiences, they will be able to actually learn from their mistakes. In work environments where mistakes are sanctioned, employees will try to hide mistakes. This leads to two problems: First, mistakes usually don't disappear – damage is done and might increase. Second, the organization itself doesn't learn from mistakes as they are not shared and discussed.

In the last chapter "MORE AGILITY THROUGH TECHNOLOGY" we aimed to show how agile management techniques can transform businesses and lead to more successful projects. These innovative management styles become even more effective by including new communication technologies.

The topic *"Maximize the chance for success: Be agile"* includes some practical cases that show how intensive client and user involvement in different project phases contributes substantially to the success of projects. The ability to adapt communication styles to different groups (e.g., clients might not understand technical specifications) and to listen actively are crucial skills when working in an agile team. Also, it is beneficial to accept change as a natural aspect of projects rather than a disturbance.

Change is an inherent part of the ICT-sector as new developments, features, and applications enter the market day-by-day. Innovations in the field of communication technology have substantially changed the ways in which we work and connect to others. They frame our relationships with others. Being successful means to be *two steps ahead* of everyone else. As the influence of mobile devices will further increase, it will be important to find appropriate strategies how to include them at work and hence improve work-relationships.

Engaging in knowledge transfer – Always a win-win situation?

During the iCom project we have engaged in various forms of cooperation: Working together in an international team of researchers, collaborating with public agencies and interest groups, building bridges to small and medium sized businesses in the ICT-sector and connecting to computer science teachers. Some connections were made at the very beginning of our project and developed to strong, institutional and personal partnerships during the last years. Other contacts were rather short-term through the workshops we provided. We learned that no matter what sort of cooperation we talk about, for a successful relationship it is necessary that both (or more) sides have a real interest and noticeable benefit from working together. This seems rational and almost needless to say – of course everyone should benefit from collaboration.

Still, in practice, when potential partners consider engaging in a project together, what happens quite often is that first of all each partner thinks about their own advantages, without considering impacts on relationships with involved partners. 'How can I get the most out of this project?' instead of 'How can everyone benefit equally (or relatively according to their share of work, investment, etc.)?' Valuing the others expertise, work and creative energy that you want them to bring into a project also means to think about their motivation to be part of the team. In the long run, it will be highly beneficial to be transparent about expectations and goals of each partner in the planning phase of a project and to allow regular exchanges about meeting these expectations.

Adhering to our experiences sketched in the various cases in this book, we would like to share with you some considerations that we have found to be helpful in building long-lasting partnerships:

- Connecting on a personal level: Institutional cooperation still comes down to collaboration between human beings.
- Allowing time for relations to develop: Strong bonds eventually grow slowly.
- Defining clear roles in cooperation: Everyone should do what they can do best.
- Clarifying expectations: What is everyone willing to invest and what are the expected outcomes?

- Creating a shared vision. Hopefully, it is one that everyone can identify with.
- Being aware of culture: Every organization, sector, country or research institution has its own culture.

As one of the goals of the iCom project was to enhance computer science teaching, we also connected to computer science teachers at secondary school level. As part of the topic "Connect the dots", you find an elaborated case about the experience of a teacher in introducing new ways of teaching (based on person-centered principles) into a rather classic-hierarchical school system. These experiences are valuable as they inspire new research in the field of education. New didactic forms that are suitable for different age groups can be elaborated drawing on these experiences. Establishing bridges and links between different stages of the educational system (primary, secondary, tertiary as well as postgraduate education) have the potential to bring along much needed innovations in the educational sector, leading to future benefits for ICT-companies through highly skilled employees. Most of the core thoughts and standpoints that we have developed in this book can be transferred from the business context to many other fields (education, public sector, industry etc.). Practice-oriented teaching includes the development of transversal personal and social skills that students will benefit from while they grow up and that will especially be helpful to them once they enter the employment market.

Becoming a constructive communicator

Before an important business event, you might have posed the following questions to yourself: "How should I act in this situation? In which way should I present myself?" Maybe, you even asked a trusted person close to you. If so, you might have gotten the following answer: "Be authentic, just be yourself!" Well, how wonderful! Just being yourself – that sounds easy! In reality, you might know very well, that being oneself can in fact be quite challenging as it presumes to know who oneself is. In the business world there are certain codes and expectations about what it means to be a professional. Acting professionally includes characteristics such as being a hard negotiator while containing oneself on a personal level and not letting emotions get in your way and effect your decisions. But emotions are an important driver for actions and realistically they can hardly be excluded from work life. From our experiences, it is therefore more helpful not trying to ignore feelings (about project developments, colleagues, clients or else) but rather trying to gain access to your natural inner emotions and become clear about them. Then, find a constructive way to make them explicit and transparent. If this inner connection with oneself has been established, you will naturally be perceived as an authentic human being, leader, co-worker, and friend. This is essential for leadership; leaders need to reflect on their personal values, what they stand for, what their principles are.

As we tried to show you with this book and as you might see now, becoming a constructive communicator is much about becoming yourself. In this way, we not only intended to support your reflective journey through your work-practices, but even more importantly to start a journey through your inner self.

Authors and Supporters

Renate Motschnig
Renate is Professor at the Faculty of Computer Science at the University of Vienna, Austria, and head of the Computer Science Didactics and Learning Research Center.
She has repeatedly been a Visiting Professor at the Computer Science Department of the University of Toronto, Canada, as well as of the RWTH-Aachen, Germany, and of the Masaryk University in Brno, Czech Republic.
Renate is author of more than 120 publications in refereed journals and conference proceedings in the fields of computer science, psychology, and education. Her research goals center around the discovery of principles and the development of techniques and tools to improve the quality of socio-technical systems.

Tomáš Pitner
Tomáš is Associate Professor at Masaryk University in Brno, Czech Republic. As a vice-dean at the Faculty of Informatics he co-established its Association of Industrial Partners in 2007. Currently, he is the head of the Lab Software Architectures and Information System at the Masaryk University. Since 2007, he is an external professor and co-supervisor at the Faculty of Computer Science of the University of Vienna, Austria.
Recently, he helps to foster innovative companies, start-ups and mentoring young firms at the Center for Research and Innovation in IT (CERIT) at Masaryk University.

Nino Tomaschek

Nino has been director of the Postgraduate Center of the University of Vienna since 2008. He has worked as Visiting Professor and Senior Research Director at the Flensburg School for Advanced Research Studies (Flensburg, Germany) and founded the research and consulting institute Sevensix-Corporate Research and Consulting in Vienna. He is University Lecturer for Philosophy of Science and habilitated on Systemic Transformation Management at the University of Augsburg where he also co-founded the Augsburg School of Innovation Coaching. Since January 2012, he is representative of the Austrian networking platform AUCEN (Austrian University Continuing Education and Staff Development Network).

Edith Hammer

Edith has worked at the Postgraduate Center of the University of Vienna since 2009 and has gained extensive experience in the field of lifelong learning and knowledge transfer. She is co-leader of the project "University Meets Industry" that strives for stronger connections between universities and practice. Edith is also a PhD-student in the field of Media and Communication Studies. Her research focuses on lifelong learning and the discursive construction of social inequality in knowledge societies.

David Haselberger

After finishing teacher training, David started to work as high school teacher in computer science and participated in academic projects on soft skills and international communication in higher education and business environments. He is deeply curious about human relationships and individual development. A major research interest is on interpersonal dynamics in leadership and teamwork.

Christina Böhm

Christina has worked as researcher and project manager at the University of Vienna since 2011. In her PhD-studies, she focuses on communication in international ICT-project environments, cultural flexibility in cross-cultural projects, and agile management approaches. Her research is highly practice-oriented due to her work experience in the IT field. Her main motivation is to raise awareness for socio-cultural impacts and plead for 'humanizing' management. In the last two years she published several articles with this emphasis.

Barbora Kozlíková

Barbora works as an Assistant Professor and project manager at the Faculty of Informatics at Masaryk University. After finishing her doctoral degree in 2011, she worked as a programmer in Home Credit International. In 2012 she returned to academia where she is a member of the Human-Computer Interaction laboratory and teaches and cooperates with students on various projects. She is also a founder of CaverSoft, a spin-off company where she is Chief Technology Officer and concentrates on marketing and sales.

Bernhard Standl

As a secondary school computer science teacher, higher education lecturer, and educational researcher, Bernhard has specialties in both the research and practice of computer science education. He aims to improve students' excitement for computer science, the preparation of future computer science teachers and the development of classroom research. In his PhD dissertation, he developed and investigated design patterns for preparing students not only in practical computer science skills but also in teamwork and cooperation, using the Person-Centered Approach.

Lucie Pekárková

Lucie has worked at the Faculty of Informatics at Masaryk University since 2006 and has gained extensive practical experience in the field of information systems, knowledge transfer, and technical support and communication. She is also a junior researcher at Masaryk University in the field of learning management systems and is deeply interested in E-learning in Process-oriented, Person-centered Knowledge Management.

Jaroslav Škrabálek

In his PhD dissertation, Jaroslav focused on modern web-based services (Web 2.0) and Mobile application development. He deepened his management skills by gaining an MBA at Dominican University in Chicago, Illinois. He is a co-founder of the first academic department designing mobile applications in the Czech Republic. Since 2010, he owns an innovative company, Takeplace, focusing on professional event management.

Martin Novák

Martin is a program manager in one of the top Forbes US technological small companies, SolarWinds. He is responsible for facilitating Scrum with international teams from the Czech Republic, the USA, and India that move web projects towards continuous delivery. He has been studying at the Faculty of Informatics at Masaryk University and he is one of the founding members of Lab of Software Architectures and Information Systems. Martin is also one of the founders of the Czech startup company Celebrio Software and holds the 2011 Ekonom Student Entrepreneur Award.

Jiří Kolář
Jiří has been engaged in practice-oriented research in Business Process Management (BPM) at the Faculty of Informatics, in which he has identified certain issues in BPM practices. He also participated on several commercial BPM projects, focusing on process analysis and consequent design of BPMs-based information systems. He worked for the company Red Hat and established industry-academia cooperation with the faculty and companies, in particular Red Hat and IBM.

Support & Layout

Andrea Schwarzová
Andrea was born in the Czech Republic and has lived in Austria since 2006. Currently, she is a student of the Slavonic studies at the University of Vienna, Austria. In spring 2012, she joined the iCom Team and got highly engaged and involved in the project's activities.

Editing

Jeffrey H.D. Cornelius-White
Language, style, and expert editing

Jakub Vémola & Zuzana Vémolová
Language editing

Illustrations

Madman

We, the iCom team, want to thank all people who supported us in our endeavor of creating this book. We especially want to thank those who helped us elaborate cases by providing their experience to us. In particular we want to thank the following people who gave input to the book: Antonín Moravec, Antonio Monteiro dos Santos, Thomas Spielhofer, Marcello Presulli, Ján Struhár, Valentin Repassy, Michael Mládek.

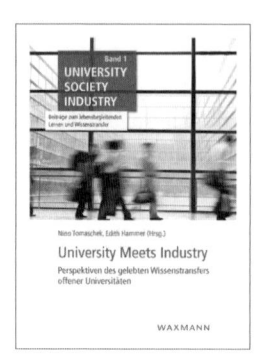

Nino Tomaschek, Edith Hammer (Hrsg.)

University Meets Industry

Perspektiven des gelebten Wissenstransfers offener Universitäten

University – Society – Industry, Band 1
2012, 276 Seiten, br., 29,90 €
ISBN 978-3-8309-2745-7
E-Book-Preis: 26,99 €

Universitäten als Orte der Wissensgenerierung und Wissensvermittlung können durch ihre Öffnung einen erheblichen Beitrag zur Hervorbringung innovativer Ideen in Unternehmen und in der Gesellschaft leisten. Gleichzeitig erhalten Universitäten durch den Austausch mit der Praxis neue Impulse für ihre Forschung. Wissenstransfer ist in diesem Sinne als wechselseitiger Prozess zu verstehen, von dem beide Seiten gleichermaßen profitieren.

Dieser Band betrachtet das Thema „Wissenstransfer" aus vielfältigen Perspektiven: Rahmenbedingungen und Strukturen für gelingende Kooperationen werden ebenso berücksichtigt wie individuelle und organisationale Lernprozesse oder die Förderung von Wirtschaftsräumen durch den gezielten Austausch zwischen Wissenschaft und Praxis.

WAXMANN

Edith Hammer, Nino Tomaschek (Hrsg.)

Vertrauen

Standpunkte zum sozialen, wirtschaftlichen und politischen Handeln

University – Society – Industry, Band 2
2013, 208 Seiten, br., 29,90 €
ISBN 978-3-8309-2874-4
E-Book-Preis: 26,99 €

Als Grundlage sozialer und wirtschaftlicher Beziehungen ist Vertrauen sowohl in zwischenmenschlichen Interaktionen als auch im organisationalen Handeln von zentraler Bedeutung. Doch wie entsteht Vertrauen und welche Konsequenzen zieht ein Vertrauensverlust nach sich?
Mit dreizehn disziplinübergreifenden Beiträgen bietet das Buch ein breites Spektrum zum Thema ‚Vertrauen' und vereint Perspektiven aus Wissenschaft und Praxis. Der Schwerpunkt des ersten Teils liegt auf psychologischen und kulturellen Aspekten der Vertrauensbildung. Der zweite Teil des Bandes geht auf Vertrauensbildung im Kontext des organisationalen Wandels ein. Herausforderungen für Politik und Wirtschaft im Zusammenhang mit Vertrauenskrisen werden im dritten Teil diskutiert.

WAXMANN